ADVOCACY ORGANIZING

Smarter Strategies, Bigger Victories

Steven E. Miller

KeepOn Press

ISBN-13: 978-1-7366016-5-5 paperbook
ISBN-10: 1736601655

ISBN-13: 978-1-7366016-6-2 e-book
ISBN-10: 1736601662

Cover design by: Rica Cabrex

Library of Congress Control Number: 2021902407
Printed in the United States of America

ALSO BY STEVEN E. MILLER
CIVILIZING CYBERSPACE: Power, Policy, and the Information Super Highway (Addison-Wesley)

CURRICULUM GUIDES from Education Development Center
Making a Living: Equal Opportunity and Affirmative Action
Immigration and Public Policy: Who Can Become An American?
Treaty Rights and Dual Status: Who Owes What to Native Americans?

BISAC: POL043000, SOC050000, SOC026040, SOC 025000

DEDICATED TO:
My parents, Betty and Bernie, whose foundation has shaped me ever since.
My wife, Sally, whose example, love, and patience are the core nutrients of my life.
My children, Andrew and Cari, whose needs and love gave me a second chance to grow up,
and daughter-in-law, Samantha, who has been such a wonderful addition;
and grandkids, Bianca, Leila, and Austin, whose healthy and happy future I hope these notes make more possible.

ACKNOWLEDGEMENTS
The original impetus for this book was the totally mistaken idea that it would be an easily assembled anthology of some of the nearly 200 essay-blogs I'd written over the past 10 years. So, my first thanks are to the many dozens of people who have read and corrected the first drafts of those posts over the years. In fact, it took five years of often interrupted work to make a few of those essays usable, fill in the huge gaps created by my evolving understanding about what I wanted to say, and then rewrite the entire thing several times. So, my second round of thanks are to the fifty or so people from around the world who offered to read early drafts in response to the email I sent to the blog mailing list. I particularly want to thank the following (in alpha order), whose enormously helpful feedback led to significant revision and restructuring: Rosalie Anders, Don Carlson, Devin Cole, Bonne DeSousa, Alex Epstein, Rachel Fichtenbaum, Terry Gleason, Judy Jacobs, Charles Knight, Helen Kobek, Jim Lerner, Ben Losordo, Michael Prokosch, Larry Rosenberg, Robert Spiegelman, Rachael Stark, Anson Stewart, Jessica Turner, and Dustin Weigl.
My latest round of feed-back friends deserve special thanks for their fast turnaround and in-depth commentary: Larry Rosenberg, Arthur McEwen, Brent Whelan, John Cumbler, Monte Pearson, Margie Alt. And my sister, Cyral, channeled our mother by being a sleuth for grammer and typos.
Special thanks go to LivableStreets Alliance co-founder Jeff Rosenberg (whose ideas were the starting point for the "Gaining Influence" chapter) as well as my friends Larry Rosenberg and George Pillsbury from whom I've learned so much.
I couldn't have done any of this without Sally's forbearance and

love. I am truely lucky.

CONTENTS

Title Page

Copyright

Dedication

CHAPTER OVERIVEW

SECTION ONE: 1

1. INTRODUCTIONS: 2

2. UNITING LOCAL AND NATIONAL: 14

SECTION II: 24

3. "MAKE GOOD TROUBLE":   25

4. EFFECTIVE ADVOCACY: 38

5. ADVOCACY AND MOVEMENTS: 49

6. CREATING MEMBERS, CHANGING BEHAVIORS: 66

SECTION III: 76

7. GAINING INFLUENCE: 77

8. INSTITUTIONAL CHANGE: 103

SECTION IV: 119

9. THEORIES OF CHANGE: 120

10. MAKING SENSE OF CONTEXT: 142

11. CULTURE, STABILITY, AND CHANGE: 150

SECTION V: 168

12. FOUNDATIONAL VISIONS: 169

13. WHY THE PUBLIC SECTOR CAN'T BE RUN LIKE A   188
BUSINESS:

14. PUBLIC-PRIVATE PARTNERSHIPS: 203

SECTION VI: 221

15. ADVOCACY AMIDST TURMOIL: 222

About The Author   239

CHAPTER OVERIVEW

*After food and shelter, the animal survival basics, the most important
thing we need is dignity – not freedom or power or wealth or status,
but a feeling of self-possession, value, and legitimate belonging in
the eyes of oneself and others.*

SECTION I: STARTING AGAIN

1. INTRODUCTIONS: People, Purpose, and Perspectives

What the book is about. Who it is for. What it doesn't cover.
Why the title is "advocacy" rather than "organizing" or "movement building."

2. UNITING LOCAL AND NATIONAL: Leveraging Reality In Today's World

Change, large and small, does happen; democratic social change
is built on real relationships. Context shapes opportunity for advocacy and organizing; we need to think and act both locally and
globally.

SECTION II: WHAT IS ADVOCACY

3. "MAKE GOOD TROUBLE": Action, Organization, Power

The core ingredients of creating change are simple and, like all
true things, enormously complicated. An overview of the advocacy world.

4. EFFECTIVE ADVOCACY: Be Prepared, Be Positive, Keep Going

Making your work create a desired result, moving from idea to
outcome, requires preparation that can be more frustrating and
slow-going than the actual campaign. But if you don't lay a good

foundation the building will inevitably topple.

5. ADVOCACY AND MOVEMENTS: Creative Anarchy and Effective Organization
Advocates frequently wish for a mass movement that will be the rising tide lifting their vision into reality. But advocacy and movements are very different phenomena and the relationship between advocacy and movements, while symbiotic, is complex.

6. CREATING MEMBERS, CHANGING BEHAVIORS: Creating Sticky Organizations And Pattern-Changing Policies
There are things you can do on your own, and a lot more things you can do with others. What brings new members and expands your circles of supporters? What makes membership "sticky?" And how does recruiting others tie into your own ability to keep going?

SECTION III: THE POLITICAL FUNCTIONS OF ADVOCACY

7. GAINING INFLUENCE: The Three Phases of Advocacy – Protest, Pushing, Partnership
Progressive advocacy tends to be an outsider effort, seeking influence by, or on behalf of, those who lack it. The purpose of organizing campaigns is to find ways to push in – to not merely stop what you don't like but to implement what you do. This requires the flexibility of cycling around the three strategic phases, working for leverage from the outside on what happens inside programs and institutions.

8. INSTITUTIONAL CHANGE: The Systemic Functions of Advocacy – Mobilizing Political Will, Ensuring Agency Capacity, Securing Permanence
To achieve significant and lasting change, advocates' increased influence needs to push society's institutions and systems through a specific set of policy and operational transformations.

SECTION IV: WORKING WITHIN LARGER CURRENTS

9. THEORIES OF CHANGE: Why Things Happen

History doesn't just happen; change has a variety of causes. But this confusing cacophony of causality can be categorized and understood – increasing advocates' ability to gain political momentum and leverage.

10. MAKING SENSE OF CONTEXT: Weaving Your Way Through Local Reality

Knowing the trends and dynamics of the immediately surrounding political and economic realities helps identify potential allies, shape immediate demands in more winnable ways, and increases the chance of riding to victory on someone else's tailwind.

11. CULTURE AND STABILITY: Majoritarian Inertia and Social Tectonics

Default social "truths" – the generally accepted frame of understanding of what is the current state of affairs, what is possible, what is unacceptable – change over time. Progressives are always hoping – and pushing – for cultural change to make their ideas more acceptable, pragmatic, realistic, and mainstream. But the shifting of our culture's crustal plates – widespread changes in consciousness and behavior – is as likely to release earthquakes as to raise up mountains.

SECTION V: STRATEGIC ISSUES

12. FOUNDATIONAL VISIONS: Community, Equality, Freedom, Democracy

Social change is more likely to occur if you can express your vision in terms of a society's historic cultural values. But our society has a range of sometimes conflicting visions and values, some of which are part of the problem rather than the source of a solution. Framing a coherent starting point requires some thought.

13. WHY THE PUBLIC SECTOR CAN'T BE RUN LIKE A BUSINESS: Universal, Democratic, Open-Ended
Business aims to be efficient, flexible, and innovative – at least in terms of pursuing profit. There is much that public (and non-profit) organizations can learn from business and much to be gained by incorporating business methods in certain situations. But government is not a business and, in fact, reduces its primary social value to the extent it narrows its operational self-evaluation to cost-effectiveness.

14. PUBLIC-PRIVATE PARTNERSHIPS: Creating Public Value through Privatizing, Contracting, and Collaboration
For-profit organizations perform much of our nation's production, distribution, and sales. Non-profits ("third sector") groups do most social services and cultural activity. Governments, even in mixed, social democratic economies, massively work with or through those organizations. But wrapping it all up under a single Public-Private Partnership label misses the large social impact different forms of those relationships can take.

SECTION VI: MOVING FORWARD
15. ADVOCACY AMIDST TURMOIL: Fights On Two Fronts
The post-Vietnam "New World Order" has collapsed. Around the globe, politicized religious fundamentalism and racist nationalism working in alliance with reactionary business leaders are opposed by progressive activists – with corporate (neo-)liberals and "back to normalcy" moderates trying to recreate a dissolving center. Even as the stakes escalate and struggles intensify, advocacy has a critical role to play in connecting people's daily reality to larger visions.

SECTION ONE:
STARTING AGAIN

Reality inevitably outruns our plans and preconceptions, forcing us to blunder forth into the stream of experience with neither a compass nor a map.
BENJAMIN SERBY, THE NATION, 9/3/18

When you are organizing a group of people, the first thing that we do is we talk about the history of what other people have been able to accomplish – people that look like them, workers like them, ordinary people, working people – and we give them the list: these are people like yourself; this is what they were able to do in their community.
DOLORES HUERTA, UNITED FARM WORKERS UNION

1. INTRODUCTIONS:
People, Purpose, and Perspectives

2. UNITING LOCAL AND NATIONAL:
Leveraging Reality In Today's World

1. INTRODUCTIONS:
People, Purpose, and Perspectives

The definition of insanity is doing the same thing over and over and expecting different results.

YOUR FAVORITE FAMOUS NAME HERE

If you're reading this, it's likely that you, too, are worried about the state of our communities, nation, and world; and that you want to learn more about how positive societal change comes about. Or perhaps you're already involved and want to understand more about what makes social change efforts effective. Welcome!

Working for improved lives and better living conditions for everyone -- including ourselves – is a good way to live. Several times, in the hit rap-musical show, *Hamilton: The Revolution*, people sing that the mid-1700s were a wonderful time to be alive. They were right: periods of dramatic and rapid transformation towards positive visions are special – engaging, meaningful, exciting – for both the participants and the society. But during the rest of the time, progress is neither inevitable nor steady.

Most of the time, established institutions do their job of protecting the status quo – meaning the interests of the rich and powerful – by reluctantly absorbing unavoidable adjustments and ignoring or crushing anything that pushes for more. Sometimes, reactionary elites roll back progress.

In the early 1960s, my first political action was picketing a Woolworths in support of Southern sit-in protesters; I was 16. In college, I did community service and worked against the US invasion of Vietnam (I also studied history and acting.) Through the 1960s and 70s I was a community organizer around tenants' unions and racism, highway construction and mass transit, war and imperialism, workplace safety and union democracy, environment and health, among other issues.

Like the revolutionaries of 1776, I still think that I was lucky to come of age at a time when so much seemed possible, when personal and world liberation seemed linked, when it felt like we were turning the gears of history. My generation participated in the successful climax of the anti-segregationist Civil Rights Movement, the start of the women's and gay movements', the anti-war movement's (admittedly temporary) halting of US military interventions, and an amazing cultural celebration of new spheres of personal freedom. It was a time of hope, joy, and important victories.

Those experiences shaped the rest of my life. They inspired me to being an activist and organizer around issues as diverse as housing and technology. Today, as global temperatures rise, I work to secure the future of our planet as much as the decency of our society. As I write this, I'm into my 70s and we are solidly into the 21st century. The most immediate development is the takeover of the Republican Party by Trump's coalition of libertarian billionaires, small business reactionaries, patriarchal religious fundamentalists, racist nationalists, and violently masculinist vigilantism. But we've also seen the re-emergence of progressive activism at both the local and national levels, with a new generation of organizers – Black and white and Latinx, male and female and other -- stepping up to take leadership. There is reason for hope as well as trepidation.

Still, big leaps don't happen without a long run-up of small steps. And those small steps require constant advocacy. Changing the world is not all-or-nothing. It moves in uneven steps, sometimes large, usually small. You spend most of your time, energy, and resources laying a foundation with frustratingly little actual worldly impact to show for it. Over the years I've learned that having some idea of how what you're doing fits into the larger world context helps you persist, makes the whole effort more likely to succeed, and makes it much easier to explain to others – including those family and friends who keep wondering why you can't stop bugging them around one issue or another.

I have no pretension of having been a major game changer in any movement, much less American society as a whole, although I'm proud to believe I contributed to some small but useful advances. I've come to understand that advocacy is necessary for democracy. It is a key way that problems are acknowledged and improvements won. It is a way to push America to take its ideals seriously. I'm proud, and happy, to have been (and to continue to be) part of that. It's never enough; but it is something.

Advocacy And Organizing

Typically, this type of book would say it was about organizing or movement building rather than advocacy. I use advocacy for several reasons. First, not everyone who supports social justice activism is an organizer. There is a broad range of valuable involvement in progressive efforts – we start as empathetic _observers_. The first big step it to become an interested _supporter_, or a low-key _participant_. Only a few people will become a consistent _activist_, a facilitating _organizer_, or a strategic _leader_. I find that saying "advocacy" allows me to talk with a broad variety of people whose efforts encompass the full spectrum from standing up for oneself to movement building. All of which, I believe, are contributing to movement in a good direction.

Second, after Barack Obama became president, the title of Community Organizer became trendy in liberal circles and began getting applied to a lot of jobs that, in my opinion, were more about social service management than progressive change – more about helping people be good recipients of social services than about changing the societal systems that were causing the problem.

Finally, advocacy feels like a more modest term than organizing. During the years that Trump and his allies were pulling American politics to the increasingly unhinged and fascistic right, it seemed important to acknowledge the narrower political space that progressives were able to work within. While the realm of possibility has expanded under the more positive atmosphere of the Biden Administration and after the Trumpites' discrediting caused by their insurrectionary riots, I decided to keep the more cautious wording as a reminder of what we may face again if the Democrats allow our society's festering inequalities and insecurities to continue.

To Be Of Use

This book is for people who want a better understanding of the ways that advocacy connects to social change, and the ways that the larger societal context shapes what is possible for advocates to accomplish. Understanding the flow of forces around you is necessary for developing effective strategies, for identifying possible allies in unanticipated places, for building sustainable and nurturing organizations. I hope it is of interest both to those doing advocacy and those wanting to understand more about social dynamics in general. My hope is that it helps you think more deeply, analytically, and usefully about the realities you need to navigate as you make strategic and tactical decisions – or at least to better understand the decisions made by others.

To be clear: this is not a "how-to" manual explaining how to run a campaign or manage an organization. It's not the curriculum for a workshop. It is mostly full of ideas: my hope is that every chapter has at last a half-dozen items that make you think. What I explore in the following pages are the topics and lessons that usually get discussed in the off-hours after the advocacy or organizational development or leadership training workshop, as you're sitting around drinking coffee or beer. These are the insights that we slowly extract from daily activity, or that we pick up from listening to more experienced or wiser people, or that we learn from our reading. I hope these notes help you better fit yourself within the range of advocacy options, some of which fit better in certain situations, and in certain of your own life stages, than others. We need to be healthy and happy as well as effective.

Recurring Themes

Each chapter echoes some combination of the following themes:

- Advocacy covers a broad spectrum. It takes a variety of forms, goes through a variety of phases, performs a variety of functions, and serves a variety of purposes from individualistically self-serving to social change movement building.
- Individuals will play different roles over the course of their lives. In fact, accepting the necessity of shifting roles as one's life circumstances and the larger societal conditions change is one of the foundations for sustained engagement.
- People who have personally suffered through the negative impacts of a problem or issue often have unique and valuable insights about its impacts and patterns. But while victims' perspectives and voices are essential, they are not usually sufficient. When seeking solutions for systemic problems, alliances with, and even leadership from, people with a variety of backgrounds is often essential for success.
- Advocacy happens within many layers of interacting and overlapping contexts: familial, community, demographic, religious, climatic, geographic, cultural, economic, political, national, and international. Advocacy is most often successful when it is pushing in the same direction as forces and trends in these surrounding contexts. However, there are also times when it is worthwhile, or simply unavoidable, to swim against the current to see what can be achieved, or to even stand alone in the Quaker tradition of "bearing witness to power."
- While often motivated by idealistic visions of radical social transformation, advocacy is inherently reformist rather than revolutionary, typically ending up with the improvement and occasionally the restructuring of the existing system rather than its overthrow. However, these victories can

be incredibly important and life-changing to those who are affected. In addition, it is sometimes possible to win "revolutionary reforms" that change the framework of public discussion and the balance of power within institutions as well as improve current conditions.

- Advocacy campaigns, community and workplace organizing, all have a symbiotic relationship with larger movements; but they are very different phenomena with distinct types of leadership, dynamics, and goals.

- In general, the most transformative social change movements combine both personal and systemic/institutional transformation; both the creation of community-level methods of mutual support and successful strategies of working within surrounding institutions.

- The bigger and more fundamental the issue, the more that success requires the eventual engagement of some sectors of the existing establishment – insiders, power brokers, and those seeking personal or corporate advantage – and even some complicity with the systems that are the source of the problems that you are working to eliminate. This tension needs to be acknowledged to be managed.

- Utopia has never and will never exist. Every society is imperfect and every victory is only partial. However, believing in – and campaigning for – the possibility of idealistic, life-changing improvement is a necessary motivational foundation for long-term effort. Strategically balancing the tension between what is envisioned and what is winnable, between when to be intransigent and when to compromise, between the motivating dream and what is actually gained, is – like the need to think three steps ahead – part of the reason for strategic planning.

Caveats

I have endless respect for the importance of deep knowledge and experience with specific issues – climate change, transportation, education, human services, or any of the other in-need-of-improvement aspects of our world. I have spent many years engaged in several of these issues. But digging into the details of any particular issue is not the purpose of this book.

Conspicuously, these notes are not a deep dive into the origins and manifestations of, or strategies to address, our society's fundamental issues of race, class, patriarchy/gender, nationalism/group identity, and family/personality. These enduring issues and their interactions deserve, and have, entire books – and movements – dedicated to their analysis and to actions dealing with them. Still, I think there are generalizable patterns common to the struggle against all of these problems; those organizing similarities are what these notes are about.

Similarly, I think much of what I discuss is relevant to the on-going debates about fashioning a national or international movement capable of winning a progressive majority in state or federal legislatures, governors or the presidency. But party building is not my topic, even though I fervently hope for such a situation and continue to participate in many efforts towards that goal.

Keeping the wheels of activism turning requires resources. People power is fundamental, but whether we like it or not, so is money. Over the past decades, right-wing groups pioneered methods of amassing huge amounts through outreach to grass-roots small donors; a financing method that the Obama and Sanders presidential campaigns built on for progressives. But both on the right and the left, big donors still play a huge role. It is a painful truth that behind nearly every major advocacy organization are one or more dedicated patrons. It is a multi-edged sword that both enables and limits social change. The politics of money is complicated and essential, and bigger than would fit in this book.

Finally, although I occasional talk about religion, these notes are not a deep dive into the philosophical and religious traditions that energize so much of advocacy by motivating outrage at injustice and hope for a better world. Religion, of course, has multiple facets. Frederick Douglas, in his *Narrative*, said, "I love the pure, peaceable, and impartial Christianity of Christ: I therefore hate the corrupt, slaveholding, women-whipping, cradle-plundering, partial and hypocritical Christianity of this land."

Still, moral principles – often uncompromisingly absolute and beyond pragmatic possibility – are the starting point for most transformative movements. Without the radical values of a movement's prophets a movement has less motivation and no compass. However, without the involvement of pragmatic deal-makers and self-interested negotiation partners within established elites, change might not occur. The more successful an advocacy campaign, the bigger the movement, the more the tension between material and moral forces must be dealt with. These notes emerge from the need to live within that tension.

What Follows

This book covers a lot of ground. The six sections slowly expand perspective and then pull back in. Section I, *Starting Again*, includes this Introduction and an overview of the national political context. Section II, *What Is Advocacy?*, discusses exactly that: what makes advocacy effective, how it relates to but remains distinct from large-scale movements, and why thinking of the process of gaining membership and supporters is most usefully framed as community-building.

Section III, *The Political Functions of Advocacy*, examines social change organizing from the perspective of working "outside the system," then describes the "inside-the-system" institutional change that such effort needs to accomplish, and ends by looking at the role of inside advocates in making those changes work and stick. Section IV, *Working Within Larger Contexts*, looks outward to the surrounding society, examining the overlapping relevance of different theories of change, the importance of working within major trends and leveraging faction-fights within the established political economy, and begins exploring how shifts in mass culture happen.

Section V, *Strategic Issues*, pulls the focus back towards the types of arguments that advocates will have to make and the kinds of proposals they will have to evaluate, and reject or support. It also points out ways that political reforms can be informed by efforts in the public health sector to change public attitudes and behaviors.

I end with Section VI, *Moving Forward*, that discusses the evolving world and national context and how it is changing the context for advocacy, movement building, and their interaction -- a topic worthy of several of its own books.

Activist Deviants Unite!

History shows that every "mass movement" is actually a minority effort. (Accept it; your cousins are right: you are a little weird!) From the American Revolution to the Civil Rights Movement to the Tea Party, social change is only embraced as "normal" by the majority after (and if) it proves successful. Today, even conservatives celebrate Martin Luther King Jr. – and then use his words to cover their opposition to further progress.

For most people, history is like a passing parade. The politically active people marching in the street are blowing their horns, singing and dancing and chanting with an enthusiasm and conviction that makes it clear they believe everyone else is about to join in. But the sidewalk observer knows that a block away, no one hears a thing other than the normal sounds of their daily life. This is not surprising, given the continuing reality of how Joan Didion described politics during the 1988 Presidential campaign:

> Access to [the official political process] is...limited to its own professionals, to those who manage policy and those who report on it, to those who run the polls and those who quote

them, to those who ask and those who answer the questions on the Sunday shows, to the media consultants, to the columnists, to the issues advisers, to those who give off-the-record breakfasts and to those who attend them; to that handful of insiders who invent, year in and year out, the narrative of public life. ("Insider Baseball", New York Review of Books)

Most people think of themselves as outside the political process, as even anti-politics. For most people, surviving the burdens of a turbulent and uncaring world with dignity, family, and occasional joy is a hard-won and life-affirming victory. But, from an activist perspective, survival is not enough. Victory comes from easing the symptoms and eliminating the causes of the world's brutality. Activists believe things can change. Being an advocacy organizer pulls you out of the flow of normal life, makes you see things from a different perspective. It can make you angry but also proud, alone but also connected. It adds to your burdens but also adds to your appreciation of human well-being – others as well as your own.

From inside the advocacy world, we know that while our band of troublemakers are a very small percentage of the overall population, we are the engine that turns the gears. Still, the hard truth about social change activism is that, while you are in the middle of doing it, it usually feels like you're accomplishing nothing, that the status quo is swallowing you like quicksand. It is only in retrospect that you realize you were a contributing pebble, however small, to the avalanche that reshaped the landscape.

But we know that even if progress is slow, it is worth working for. Advocacy is a way of helping others. It is also a way to help ourselves – being active is, for me, a way to feel hopeful in a difficult world, a way to connect to people with shared values, a way to personally learn and grow and feel I'm leaving things a little better than they would otherwise be.

In *The Cold Millions*, best-seller novelist, Jess Walker has the "rebel girl," Elizabeth Gurley Flynn, ruminate after being nearly killed by business-paid thugs at an Industrial Workers of the World event, that "Men sometimes say to me: 'You might win the battle, Gurley, but you'll never win the war.' But no one wins the war. Not really. I mean, we're all going to die, right? But to win a battle now and then? What more could you want?"

History Is Now

While my own core values and hopes have remained steady across my adult life, my situation and the surrounding realities of the world have gone through many changes, both positive and disastrous. I remain focused on the challenge of moving towards democracy, equity, environmental sustainability, multicultural and interpersonal respect, community, and long-term collective well-being that define the type of world I want to leave for my grandchildren. These are long-term, continuing issues whose realization will require a radical restructuring of power, a societal prioritization of people over profit and caring relationships over dominance, and a rejection of racism and institutional discrimination of all kinds. I have been an activist my whole life, and while I once thought that these changes were imminent, I now doubt that they will happen in my lifetime, if ever. But that doesn't change my commitment or willingness to keep trying, my refusal to give up, my perhaps irrational hopefulness that we can win some gains.

My father, a history teacher, used to say that every important idea we have can be traced back to the ancient Greeks (and today people would say the Nubians). So I doubt that anything I've written is totally new or unique. But I hope my way of discussing and assembling this material helps others learn a bit more of what they need to know to make a difference, to understand a bit more about where their efforts fit within the larger processes of social change, to think more deeply and effectively about turning values and concerns into action, and to avoid a few of the innumerable stupid mistakes that every advocacy and organizing effort stumbles through.

Find your own way through these pages: skim some sections, jump around, take notes, read it through, whatever. And then talk with others about what you've read – turning ideas into strategy is a group process that grows best when rooted in the ground you stand on. People most comfortable with 110-character Tweeted abbreviations will probably find my broad explorations of issues a bit of a slog. Even worse, in order to give each Section some stand-alone value a small amount of repetition was necessary. But I hope it's worth it. I'm also aware that political writing is partly a pretentiously hopeful belief in the power of one's words to make a difference in the world, or to at least help increase other people's understanding of that world. I plead guilty. Please get in touch if you have questions or comments or your own thoughts and experiences to share. I can be reached via KeepOnPress@gmail.com

Steven E. Miller 2021

2. UNITING LOCAL AND NATIONAL:
Leveraging Reality In Today's World

Give me a place to stand and a lever strong enough, and I will move the world.

ARCHIMEDES, 250 BCE

This book was written to help grassroots advocates and organizers better analyze the structures of power that surround them and the organizational strategies they must choose among to successfully facilitate progressive social change.

The first drafts of this book were written during the second Obama Administration. Despite the first African-American president's cultural significance and personal decency, his business liberalism had increased inequality and fostered frustration among the remaining Civil Rights, feminist, anti-war, and youth movements that had originally energized his rise. His finance-friendly policies had also allowed Alt-right racism to position itself as the vehicle for expressing the enormous anger at being left behind, being treated contemptuously by those doing better, felt by many middle-class Americans, especially in rural and rust-belt areas -- communities suffering from lost jobs and declining living conditions. Facing Hillary's expected continuation of New Democratic globalism, the challenge for grassroots progressive organizers was how to support mainstream Democrat's positions against discrimination while opposing their economic policies.

The next set of drafts staggered through the shock waves of Trump's encouragement and unification of previous marginal forces into a powerful movement. The Trumpite coalition's increasingly radicalized leadership – with at least the initial support of much of the nation's corporate elite seeking tax cuts and deregulation -- took over the Republican Party and reshaped the entire American political landscape from town committees to the Congress. They are anti-government, white nationalist, violently masculinist, and religiously revanchist. Building on Obama's nurturing of business revival, the Trump administration stoked the stock market, reduced unemployment, and loudly promoted American manufacturing. Proclaiming that, at every level of human life, our first priority must be ourselves, the call for restoration of lost wellbeing had enormous appeal in a world that felt increasingly dangerous and people's previous status increasingly insecure. If the Covid-19 pandemic hadn't pulled the rug out from the economy, Trump might have won a second term.

Triumphant

If nothing else, Donald Trump's presidency and the continuing power of the forces he encouraged and brought together have taught more of us what people of color, other marginalized communities, and vulnerable working-class families of all backgrounds have always known: our economy is brutally non-egalitarian, a rising tide lifts some boats and swamps many others; our civility and charity is very thinly applied; our democracy is fragile. Violent opposition to insecurity or change, as well as a turn to authoritarian governance and leaders are not aberrations of liberal capitalism, but inherent always lurking currents that flood into visibility during periods of stress -- currently caused by the inability of our profit-seeking market-dominated societies to meet the needs of its population. Trump may, or may not, personally fade away into Twitter twilight. But the forces he brought to light were always there, waiting to be called forth, and having swelled into their current power, will not go away.

And it isn't just a national aberration: Trumpism was merely the American version of a world-wide phenomenon. Authoritarian movements based in right-wing populism had also taken power in Turkey, Israel, India, Brazil, Russia, Hungary, Poland, and was increasingly influential in the UK – all joining the reactionary or corrupt dictatorships already in power in much of Africa, Latin

America, and the Arab world. It felt like the world was entering a new era, as distinct and holistic as the post-World War II Cold War prosperity, the post-Vietnam War loosening of super power control, and the post-Soviet New World Order of capitalist globalism.

I struggled to keep up with ideas about how organizers could deal with this rapidly escalating slide towards an American version of fascism, environmental disaster, and barbaric survivalism – and eventually stopped writing.

The Current Challenge

The upswelling of positive energy created by the massive and successful effort to dump Trump has brought a fresh dose of progressive promises and a chance to finish this book. Biden's empathetic decency, safety net improvements, and surprisingly strong proposed reforms will -- if successfully passed and implemented -- strip off some layers of the Trumpist coalition. The amazing Democratic double win in the Georgia Senate runoffs has allowed many impactful changes in environmental/climate policy, in our woefully porous safety nets, in improving government revenues and administration, and reducing the meritocracy-denying discrimination affecting women, people of color, LBGTQ, and immigrants. These are important victories that will make a difference in people's lives.

The continuing response to the #metoo and Black Lives Matter protests will also have an effect on our national institutions and their decision-making networks. It's likely that there will be increased recruitment of individuals from previously marginalized groups into institutional elites. The personal cost of their entry is likely to be the espousal of business-friendly values and behaviors, but even so their presence, by expanding demographic representation in visible positions of authority, is a step towards a culture of inclusive national community.

Still, unless carried to their full systemic implications -- as does not currently seem likely to happen – even these positive steps will not permanently change the hardships faced by the majority of marginalized groups, nor eliminate the underlying structural dynamics that perpetuate their exploitative treatment. Furthermore, Biden's own Clinton-Obama legacy of financial globalism and militarized internationalism, coupled with domestic corporate priorities, Republican opposition, and the continued cautious "moderation" of the majority of Democrats, sets real limits to what he can accomplish. So much of what is wrong about the world comes from core institutional practices developed over time and now mutually re-enforcing on a multi-generational, systemic level. As Black Lives Matter founder, Alicia Garza, says in *The Purpose of Power*,

> *Police do not abuse Black communities because there are good people and bad people on police forces throughout the nation – police abuse Black communities because the system of policing was designed in a way that makes that abuse inevitable.*

So, the questions originally motivating this book remain: What do we need to know and do to mobilize enough power to make positive change in our institutions and culture? How do we push the liberals in power to go beyond their cautious reforms to make more fundamental changes to the well-being – both material and perceived – of the majority of Americans? And, at the same time, how do we work with liberals – and moderates as well -- to defend and expand access to our political system in the face of increasingly reactionary and racist conservative attacks? How do we acknowledge the pain and injustice suffered by marginal peoples while building a movement broad enough to win power, majoritarian enough to be democratic?

LOOKING FOR LEVERAGE

The modern Tea Party, mostly led by small businessmen but spread nationally by Koch family financed networks, gained veto power over Republican candidates by being willing to let Democrats defeat any GOP hopeful who did not swear allegiance to their libertarian positions -- a tactic Trump continues to effectively use to control the party. The mirror-reverse of this is the left-wing anti-electoral stance that says "they're all the same" and sees all officials as enemies. (Even worse than abstentionism are those who echo the mid-1920s position of the German Communist Party that focused most of its energy on defeating the reformist Social Democrats under the slogan "after Hitler, us" – we all know where that led.)

In the current circumstances, the last thing progressive activists should do is further undermine the remaining public support for what democracy we have left. Instead, progressives must push to expand and deepen democratic control over ever-more aspects of our policy-making and markets. This will require local organizing, lobbying, mass mobilizations, and militant non-violent civil disobedience -- as well as endless and patient electoral work.

It should not include resurrecting the 1960s myth of armed revolution to overthrow state power. Trump's Capital-invasion mob failed to achieve to achieve any of their immediate goals even with the support of the sitting President, most of the state and national level leadership of the Republican Party, significant numbers of police and military people, and perhaps as much as a quarter of the American population. Violent, armed uprising isn't going to work. Not to mention that the friendly treatment of the coup insurrectionists by police and army would not be repeated should African-American or leftist insurgents were involved. Few would walk away unharmed.

On the other hand, neither should progressives give in to the mainstream Democrats who try to blame their down-ballot losses, despite often spending more money than their Republican opponents, on progressives' "inflammatory rhetoric." Progressives have to keep insisting that it's the liberals' timid policies and lack of deep local engagement around issues of daily concern to the majority of people that is the real problem.

An alternative approach is Bernie Sander's decision to stand as an independent progressive but work in alliance with liberals; to run for President within the Democratic primaries but to use his momentum to create and then spin-off autonomous national organizing networks such as Our Revolution. This is partly a recognition of the ineffectiveness of third parties in recent American history as well as the relative weakness of progressive forces. (The spread of Instant Runoff or Ranked-Choice Voting may reduce that problem.) But it's also an acknowledgement that liberals are not the primary enemy – that it is better for democracy and social progress to put liberals in office rather than conservatives: Obama may have served Wall Street but he didn't call forth armed vigilantes!

We also have to re-examine our tendency to over nationalize our politics. It's true that the federal government sets the tone for the nation. Removing Trump from the White House will change what is possible at state, municipal, and community levels. But an obsession with Washington obscures the fact that movements are built from the bottom up. We need to balance our upward gaze towards Washington with solidarity and mutual aid in our communities.

"Think global, act local" is a good corrective to our tendency to over nationalize politics. But it's not really accurate. We need to simultaneously build locally-grounded campaigns to fight for locally specific change at the same time we build national movements for systemic transformation. Town hall and DC – both are necessary targets if either is to succeed. We must find ways to fully entwine local fights around the immediate problems in people's lives with national demands: jobs, food, housing, health, safety, policing, the environment, schools, and more. And that national politics must create programs that facilitate local power.

A bottom-up, locally-relevant issues approach also affects language. We have to express our core values of democracy, equity,

supportive community, mutual aid and respect in ways appropriate to our everyday struggles and our concerned neighbors.
As Theda Skocpol and Caroline Tervo point out in their powerful
critique of national Indivisible ("Resistance Disconnect", *American Prospect*, 2/4/21):

> *Even when their concerns parallel national priorities, local
> activists usually approach issues in less ideologically hectoring
> ways—for example, by holding a community forum on prac-
> tical environmental issues or engaging local churchgoers in
> discussions of racial justice and refugee assistance.*

And, perhaps, we have to go even deeper. Civil rights leader
Bob Moses and others point out that the most transformative
movements are those in which the collective fight against societal injustice leads participants to change themselves, to learn
about their own strength and creativity and ability to love. And
this is most likely to happen when the values and vision of the
movement is deeply humanitarian, meaningfully utopian, and
politically astute enough to win incrementally worthwhile and
symbolic victories while never forgetting the ultimate ideal.

Reconnecting With Our Roots

Political analyst Eitan Hersh points out that real engagement, real base building, is rooted in community service, that
our leverage comes from the interaction of our local organizing
with our national goals:

> *If you went to a Black Lives Matter protest this summer, which
> a lot of people did, someone at the front of that protest prob-
> ably gave a speech that went something like this, they said,
> "Thank you for coming. This is step one, what we really need
> you to do is come to the city hall meeting, come to the town hall
> meeting, come when we go before the board, the council, we
> recommend these five concrete things. We need you to show up
> and back us up because it's hard to make these changes and we
> need you to come be there for us."*

> *So, for the random person who went to a Black Lives Matter*

protest, the question is, was that protest the beginning and the end of their engagement? Or was it a gateway into showing up... working with other people to achieve concrete goals [in our communities]? (Politics is for Power, How to Move Beyond Political Hobbyism, Take Action, and Make Real Change)

And there are endless issues to dig into. At least 7.8 million people have fallen into poverty in recent years, the biggest plunge in six decades; 85 million Americans say they have had trouble paying basic household expenses, including food and rent; there are roughly 10 million fewer jobs now than there were the previous year. Childcare. Addictions. Homelessness. Violence. Closed social service programs and non-profits. Medicines. Eviction. "Sometimes," says the Rev. Richard Gibson, "it feels like we're losing our grip on civilization." *(NYTimes, 1/2/2021)*

Intertwining national and community issues is vital because people are more likely to have their ideas and behaviors changed through interaction with people they know and trust -- especially when those people are helping them overcome obstacles in their own lives. People are more likely to take a stand on national issues if they see them as an extension of things they've fought for at home. This is well known by the growing megachurches with their plethora of community-building mutual-support groups, and by many far-right groups – as recently as 2018 the North Carolina Ku Klux Klan was going around to opioid addicts and saying, "you have an opioid addiction, but it's not your fault. We're here to help you."

Fortunately, right wingers aren't the only ones to understand this reality. During the Great Depression left-wing union activists built social service and cultural extensions of their workplace organizing. In the 1960s the Black Panthers created free breakfast programs as well as protection from the police. During the early 2021 Georgia Senatorial runoffs, when an amazing double victory transformed national political possibilities, local organizers went out to meet their community where they are - at grocery stores, malls, skating rinks, bus stops, boutiques, faith spaces, and coffee shops. Black Voters Matter organized a 12-day tour bus across the state providing food and other services while they registered voters or brought people to the polls. Their Thursday "Collard Green Caucuses" feed more than 9,000 families on top of the 10,000 plus families the organization had already provided food during the holiday season – using food donated by local Black farmers. The Black Male Voter Project and the New Georgia Project put together huge drive-in rallies at malls and amphitheater parking lots. The Georgia Working Families Party ran parties for holiday-returning college students urging them to register and vote.

This is not charity; it is movement building. Movements grow from organizing and from organizations. As veteran organizer Arnie Graf notes in *Lessons Learned*, working our way through the many struggles ahead will require resources that only organizations can provide: local knowledge, deep relationships, mobilization and communication expertise, experience with conflict and negotiations, and ways to develop new leaders. Says Deepak Bhargava in *Of Ducks and Democracy*, (The Forge website, 12/8/20):

> We're fond of chanting at militant demonstrations, that 'this is what democracy looks like," but tough front-porch conversations – less ecstatic to be sure – are also what democracy looks like. The unflashy, careful, disciplined, person-by-person relational work that good organizations teach matters just as much as the scale of contact.... High-quality, rigorous, relationship-based organizing is what changes people's minds and moves them to act.

This process builds on endless individual decisions and actions. But to be part of a base-building process, these cannot happen in isolation. They have to be part of a longer-term, strategically smart development of local organizations and national movements. Improving people's immediate lives and the world requires navigating through the conflicting currents of power flowing within and between all the layers of society. Even if you are a fervent believer in bottom-up people power, your chances of success are increased by knowing the various interests of competing factions of the powerful, the way international trends are changing the options available to society's elites, how technological developments are upsetting existing industries.

The trick is to remember that the longest journey begins with a single step, and that those steps happen right in front of you.

SECTION II:
WHAT IS ADVOCACY

You may never know what results come of your actions, but if you do nothing, there will be no results.

ATTRIBUTED TO MAHATMA GANDHI

3. "MAKE GOOD TROUBLE":
Action, Organization, Power

4. WHAT MAKES FOR EFFECTIVE ADVOCACY:
Be Prepared, Be Positive, Keep Going

5. ADVOCACY AND MOVEMENTS:
Creative Anarchy and Effective Organization

6. CREATING MEMBERS, CHANGING BEHAVIORS:
Creating Sticky Organizations and Pattern-changing Policies

3. "MAKE GOOD TROUBLE":
Organization, Action, Power

I am no longer accepting the things I cannot change. I am changing the things I cannot accept.

ANGELA DAVIS

Power concedes nothing without a demand. It never did and it never will.

FREDERICK DOUGLAS

Advocacy comes in many forms. But social change advocacy requires organization, action, and power. It also requires believing that problems can be solved.

Belief in the possibility of change, of improvement in your own and other's lives, is a vital stepping stone for taking on the effort and risks of action. Hope. It's true that sometimes people are pushed into desperate action by what's happening around them. But a collapsing sense of possibility more typically leads to personal and group self-destruction, as seen in the rise of addiction and suicide in declining communities. Hope has a more positive effect. Belief in the possibility of change helps you work for it.

Advocates, by definition, seek change. Certain kinds of change start internally. As an individual you can "be the change you wish to see" by modeling new behaviors that inspire others, thereby making your action a form of small-scale public education. Although personal growth is an important pillar of support for long-term activism, social change advocacy is not really a self-help enterprise. Social change occurs when you seek change outside yourself, in the surrounding society. The purpose of that kind of advocacy is to make good things happen in the world, which happens, in Civil Rights veteran and Congressman John Lewis' words, when you "make good trouble."

What Is Advocacy

Advocacy can be done individually. But social change advocacy is usually the organizational kind. Organized advocacy starts with raised awareness, focused research, an examination of alternatives, and tentative proposals. Advocates identify problems and unmet needs. They frame the issue in a way that emphasizes the values and interests at stake, attracts support, and describes a path to possible solutions. They identify challenges to the appropriate implementation of those solutions. They help mobilize the people and resources needed to overcome barriers. They monitor the results of their efforts and reforms and push for incremental improvements, as well as address the political and material impact of the inevitable unintended (and often unforeseen) consequences, whether good or bad.

Organized advocacy is the mobilization of resources and power to address societal problems. It can create conditions for solving many individuals' problems; more significantly, it can increase the influence of those previously excluded from decision-making and operational processes, particularly those most adversely affected by the problem. Winning almost always requires getting a program, organization, or system to do something that it wouldn't otherwise have done; to overcome inertia and resistance to deviating from business as usual, to upset some interest.

Much advocacy is simply a fight against institutional and cultural inertia, the difficulty or unwillingness to deviate from past patterns of practice and thought even when obviously inefficient, unsustainable, or even self-defeating. Bringing institutional practices up to date can require policy and operational improvements, or a total transformation, or even an entirely new organization with a new mission and operational dynamic. But this seldom happens easily or without resistance. Sometimes, the advocates' concerns are not shared by a sufficiently large (or sufficiently powerful) percentage of the larger society.

Sometimes, established elites fear that change would diminish their hold on status, wealth, or power. Sometimes, a key group of non-elite stakeholders have become used to their conditions or are unwilling to risk losing what they have, no matter how inadequate.

The hard reality is that neither belief nor effort guarantees success. There are times that the surrounding context is simply too hostile, its layers of power too misaligned, for you to get enough traction to move forward. Even when successful, campaigns seldom end up with the results that advocates initially envisioned. You can do everything right and still fall short of your vision. These are painful possibilities to contemplate, but activism is still usually a life worth living, a life well lived. Your satisfaction must come from your own – and your community's – appreciation of the values you've expressed, the struggles you've contributed to, and the lives you've affected, your own as well as others'.

THE ADVOCACY SPECTRUM

Advocacy has many nuances. *Benefit advocacy* works for the specific needs of individuals (including yourself), groups, or constituencies. *Mission-driven* advocacy focuses on the problem rather than the beneficiary. This is often motivated by moral, religious, or ethical principles – whose adherents describe their groups as being *value based*. *Issue-oriented* advocacy focuses on changes in policies, procedures, structures, and systems related to a specific area of concern – reproductive rights, housing, special needs education, disability access. All this sometimes spills into progressive *social change* or *social justice* organizing, in which the goal is to raise society's floor in general, to broaden the ranks of those who share in the exercise of every type of power.

Often, the demands of advocates imply values and visions with implications beyond the particular reforms being pushed. However, few people start out wanting to overthrow their entire existence and world. They just want something better. Even though the leadership of reform movements often is (or be-comes) more radical than the average participant, advocacy al-most always starts with the public presumption that change is possible within some version of the existing society. No matter how militant its actions, and no matter how idealistic its vision, advocacy inherently starts as a push for reforms rather than revolution.

Still, social justice advocacy can easily end up requiring us to confront our society's deepest institutional and structural issues: racism, patriarchy, our corporate-dominated economy, and the disproportionate influence of the rich and powerful on our political system. The most progressive efforts focus on "revolutionary reforms" that increase the opportunities for per-sonal growth and collective power of the oppressed, repressed, or exploited in relation to those "above" them in ways that set the stage for additional future advances. At this level, advocacy can turn into movement-building.

Organization: Infrastructure To Support Out-reach

One distinguishing advantage of organized advocacy is its ability to sustain effort through the full cycle of Protest, Pushing, and Partnership – preventing or stopping what you don't like, pushing for adoption of what you want, and then working with the implementing agencies to make sure it is done well: moving on if things go well, or finding the energy and re-sources to repeat the whole process if things go wrong. (More on this in later chapters.) It is hard, if not impossible, to do this year after year, campaign after campaign, as an individual or even as an informal group.

Being organized is different from being an organization. While the former implies efficiency, the latter requires effective admin-istration and financial stability. Advocacy needs both. True: or-ganizations require a lot of work simply to maintain and can feel like a wasteful divergence from focusing on the organization's real purpose. But advocacy organizations ignore administration at their peril. Setting up by-laws, written HR policies, careful monitoring of cash flows against conservative budgets, detailed workplans for all staff, professionally done tax and reporting forms – these are tedious and complicated. But organizations that ignore this internal infrastructure end up in crisis or collapse.

A transportation advocacy I helped start, LivableStreets Alliance, made becoming a "well-oiled machine" one of its initial strategic priorities worthy of effort and money. It was worth it – a proper degree of organizational formality can support longer term efforts beyond the scope of any particular person or informal network. Activists come and go; organizations can endure.

COMMUNICATION BOTH OUTWARDS AND INWARDS

The second essential type of organizational infrastructure advocacy needs is communication systems. Advocates need both broadband and narrow-casting outreach. Different groups often need different channels and different messages. However, in this age of video permanence, it is vital to never say anything to one group that you would have to deny if it was more widely known.

Communication is as important internally as externally. Members, too, need to be bathed in vision – a value-embodying narrative describing a believable strategy that leads to personal and societal growth valuable enough to inspire effort or even sacrifice. This is what gains the long-term allegiance of members' hearts and minds as well as appeals to their self-interest.

Action: Mobilizing People, Influencing Decisions

Advocacy starts with people coming together and the spread of motivating information. Ideas and energy are vital but not enough. Lawyers are called advocates because they speak for others, but even they seek to achieve something beyond the words. Success requires having the momentum and power to actually implement the desired change: visible change in individual and social reality. Success comes from action.

Even so, advocacy is almost always the glacial accretion of small steps, both in process and result. Even the biggest leaps take off from a long runway of incremental advances – and defeats. Even the biggest movements grow out of ideas repeated at meeting after meeting, comment letters sent and then revised and resent by someone else and then by someone else again, phone call after phone call. Although memory and media often conflate the years of effort into a single climactic moment, in reality the larger and more transformative the goals being pursued, the less likely that success is the result of a single dramatic action. There is no single fulcrum stable enough and no single lever long enough to move the human world with one push. But action builds momentum; action creates its own tailwind.

PORTFOLIO MANAGEMENT

Folk wisdom teaches us not to put all our eggs in one basket. Financial experts say that investors should spread their money across a portfolio of at least five asset types – and then expect one to fail, three to break even, and only one to be a real winner. Advocacy organizations need a similar approach to risk management. The greater the organization's resources the greater its flexibility in developing a portfolio of high-level goals, issues related to those goals, campaigns within each issue, strategies within each campaign, and activities to implement each strategy.

Furthermore, given the never-ending need, you can never do enough. However, the reality is that you can't do everything; you can't even do most things. Prioritization is vital. Advocates need to clearly separate their core issues from all the other "good things" they'd like to see happen. A key step is to create a hierarchy of action. Some issues and activities you should simply _monitor_ to stay aware of what's going on. Some you should _endorse_ but maintain a relatively low level of engagement: being "paper" co-sponsors and alerting your membership about events; signing-on to letters or petitions; but not organizing things.

Some efforts you should actively *participate* in, often as part of larger coalitions: allocating a limited amount of staff or volunteer time; contributing ideas or giving feedback about goals, strategies, and campaigns; attending (but not leading) coalition committees; writing your own letter of support or endorsement around issues; inviting speakers to your meetings; giving prominence in your newsletter to issue-related events and urging attendance; helping organize particular events; but not taking on responsibility for overall decision-making. The most important efforts are those that you help *lead*, perhaps even initiate. Those are signature campaigns that define your organization, and into which you must put all you've got. For these you take responsibility for helping decide on goals and strategy, shaping and organizing campaigns, events, and communications.

But even when your organization leads, you must distinguish between different levels of organizational effort. *Events* are one-time happenings. A *project* is a relatively short-term series of events and activities. But the core of the program has to be a series of mission-related and organizational-defining *campaigns* that draw upon all the resources and contribute to all the critical needs of the organization.

Power

Advocacy starts with the creation and spread of ideas and culture; it gathers strength through activism and public support; and it gains influence through the leveraging of its organizational assets. But the focus of all this effort is usually action by others, by decision-makers. Convincing or compelling institutions to take a desired action by influencing the people with power over or within the institution is the essence of advocacy.

It is sometimes difficult to find the focus of power in a situation; there often are a large number of players and forces involved.

Working through the complexity to find sufficient leverage can take an enormous amount of advocacy work and time to achieve even the most minuscule reforms. You may not to have to take on the entire power structure or deal with every aspect of discriminatory effect. In fact, there are always some possible partnerships with some sectors of the business world, some factions of the ruling elites, some groups within the upper classes. "Power mapping" is one way to find these leverage points – linking key decision-makers with those who influence them, then with those who influence that inner circle, and expanding until you find access points. Still, centralized or diffuse, it takes power to affect the powerful. Advocates can use a wide variety of organizing modes and strategies to acquire it.

Modes Of Organizing

Activism outside the electoral or workplace arenas is usually called "community organizing." Saul Alinsky, author of Reveille for Radicals and Rules for Radicals, is generally considered the founding father of modern advocacy-oriented community organizing. Since then, a variety of modes of advocacy have developed. Nearly all current organized advocacy involving low-income and working families incorporates many Alinsky ideas, most going beyond Alinsky's non-partisan and anti-electoral limits. The most direct lineage is expressed in *Grievance-based* organizing that pulls neighborhoods together around common complaints. The Association of Community Organizations for Reform Now (ACORN) had a national presence, growing over 40 years to nearly a half-million members. Its effectiveness in mobilizing low-income working families from different racial and cultural backgrounds to register and vote earned it the hatred of ascendant right-wing groups who, in 2009, were able to use a (subsequently shown to be false) charge of voter fraud to crush its national organization. Many state and local organizational descendants are still active, however.

Service-based organizing starts by organizing mutual-aid groups or providing needed assistance, using that as a way to meet people, gain their trust, and helping them see the possibility of group rather than individual action. Cesar Chavez and Dolores Huerta started by providing services to migrant farm laborers and their families in California, where low wages and oppressive working conditions left them in desperate need. They then built on the connections and legitimacy they had earned to organize the United Farm Workers union, moving from dealing with symptoms to confronting the causes of their members' problems.

Interest-group activism tries to make the needs and demands of its constituency visible and powerful within the swirling mix of interests in American society. This fits in with how most political leaders see their own jobs – having to balance the competing requests coming from all directions, to whom attention is paid according to the politician's own beliefs, the requesting group's level of support from influential people and institutions, as well as the group's ability to influence the politician's chances of re-election.

The most political advocacy positions itself as part of a *progressive coalition*. They seek to pull together people and groups from a variety of have-not sectors while framing their demands in ways that hopefully seem legitimate and beneficial to a broad swath of the population. Class-based groups see income, job characteristics, and culture as key starting points for solidarity. Identity politics holds that if society oppresses or exploits a person based on a particular aspect of their self – skin color, gender, country of origin, disability, etc. – then that will be the person's primary self-identity and therefore an inescapable starting point.

We have painfully learned from past experiences that class-based organizing, no matter how broadly based, can easily ignore the many other ways that people are hurt and their potential growth thwarted unless it is infused with a deep consciousness of and willingness to fight the solidarity-destroying effects of cultural and societal oppressions. We have also learned that identity-based movements can easily become self-absorbed, convinced of the absolute centrality of their own struggle to the point of either seeing everyone else as the enemy or their needs as more important than anyone else's. The mass movements of the future will be those that find ways of meaningfully combining the two strategies.

Clicks And Communication: Digital Activism

Social media is the newest mode of advocacy and organizing. The initial rollout of significant new technologies unleashes utopian hopes (and fears) of its transformational power: the printing press, steam engines, trains, electricity, cars, television. Digital communications and social media are no exception. In the advocacy world, fax machines were seen as key to the (temporary) success of the Chinese students' pro-democracy protests in Tiananmen Square. Facebook was seen as instrumental for the Arab Spring and the (temporary) collapse of several Middle Eastern dictatorships. More recently, online activism has captured headlines, allowing people to proclaim their support for an issue and communicate that to decision-makers through a simple click on a "Like" button or on a petition sign-up tab.

Perhaps most powerfully, the Internet can help connect otherwise isolated people with similar interests from around the world, allowing them to share information and strengthen their connections. And on the basis of that shared identity, online communication can stimulate further action – an email, postal letter, or phone call to a decision-maker's office or (best of all) attendance at a meeting or participation in an event.

(Unfortunately, it can also help isolated child molesters, racists, and other haters or abusers find each other as well as create markets for what they seek. So far, despite Trump's criticisms of Facebook and Twitter, the most obvious political effect of social media has been to provide tools for far-right and racist networks previously excluded from mainstream liberal and conservative outlets.)

Online communications allow enormous, low-cost distribution: people can be both producers and consumers of information and culture. Messages can "go viral" and quickly reach millions of people. It is possible to inform people about incidents that the major media is ignoring – the way that Twitter posts brought attention to the police killings in Ferguson. It can show that an opinion or demand has wide support. In repressively anti-union West Virginia, the groundbreaking teachers' strike in 2018 was organized via Facebook. The massive "text-activism" and auto-mated personal phone calls organized to help Democrats regain control of the U.S. House of Representatives in 2018 played at least some role in the huge voter turnout and may have helped tip the balance in some close districts – even if hugely annoying to the overloaded recipients.

Occasionally, online messaging can even raise money – as was spectacularly demonstrated by the ALS Ice-Bucket Challenge and Trump's Tweets. (However, a recent study shows that very few issue-oriented social media appeals for funds solicit much response beyond the personal networks of the poster.) It can expose a local injustice to broader exposure in a "naming and shaming" process that can embarrass perpetuators to take cor-rective action. (However, groups proud of their divergent values can hijack the process to brag about their extreme actions and publicize their cause the way Jihadist groups have done with their YouTube videos of beheadings, stonings, and mass mur-ders.)

MEDIA IS THE MESSAGE
Now that the novelty of social media has waned, its strengths and limitations are becoming clear. Digital communications have vastly increased our ability to communicate and do certain tasks. But technology as a whole has not and will not create, con-trary to the prediction nearly half a century ago by media futur-

ist Marshall McLuhan, a "condition of universal understanding and unity." In fact, the primary effects have been in the opposite direction: It is unlikely that today's Alt-Right fascists would have grown as rapidly or taken over the Republican Party so effectively without the new media. The creation of entrapping media niches surrounds people with endlessly reinforcing and narrowing perspectives in an artificial-intelligence-empowered, deliberately addictive, infotainment, selling-focused alternative to a thoughtful, fact-based world – not to mention face-to-face intimacy.

It has also catalyzed more rapid monopolization than any previous technology. Centralizing and monopolizing control over commercial production, distribution, and sales while creating a panopticon nightmare of potentially repressive data collection about individuals. Economic concentration brings political influence and democratic distortions. A handful of suddenly gigantic corporations now control huge portions of our lives. It is difficult to conduct business, interact with others, or participate in cultural events in Western countries without entering the world of US-based FANGAMI (Facebook, Amazon, Netflix, Google/Alphabet, Apple, Microsoft, IBM) and globally through Chinese-based BATX (Baidu, Alibaba, Tencent, and Xiaomi). The "advantages of scale" act more quickly and decisively in this industry than in any other.

Most fundamentally, the speed and reach of the new communication technologies, augmented with unprecedentedly easy data gathering and Artificial Intelligence analysis, has created the all-enveloping "attention economy" predicted by scientist Michael Goldhaber in the mid-1980s and dramatized in the film The Social Dilemma. In an attention economy, the ability to capture people's attention is the primary currency in the marketplaces of business, politics, and culture. In a recent *New York Times* interview with reporter Charlie Warzel, Goldhaber says:

When you have attention, you have power, and some people

will try and succeed in getting huge amounts of attention, and they [will] not use it in equal or positive ways." ... [He said that] it has disproportionate benefits for the most shameless among us.... Nuanced policy discussions, he said, will almost certainly get simplified into "meaningless slogans" in order to travel farther online, and politicians will continue to stake out more extreme positions and commandeer news cycles.... [He saw] Mr. Trump — and the tweets, rallies and cable news dominance that defined his presidency — as a near-perfect product of an attention economy. (I Talked to the Cassandra of the Internet Age, *2/4/2021*)

From an advocacy perspective, we've learned that there is a big difference between gaining attention and having an impact. Increasing the number of views or clicks usually requires utilizing the same sensationalist and short-attention-span manipulations that commercial media uses, which blurs the difference and melts advocacy appeals into the mush of quickly forgotten cultural consumption. Capturing eye-balls is not the same thing as provoking thought, much less changing behaviors. The fact that more people know about police murders of African-Americans hasn't, by itself, stopped cops from continuing to kill.

Social and other media, like all communications, can be a spur to action. But we are still learning how to use it.

4. EFFECTIVE ADVOCACY:
Be Prepared, Be Positive, Keep Going

Do what you can, where you are, with what you have.
THEODORE ROOSEVELT

Almost everyone wishes the world were different in one way or another. But creating that difference requires effective action, which comes in different forms, all of which, to be maximally successful, require enormous preparation. The most effective advocacy runs through a series of intensive steps even before what is usually thought of as "advocacy" actually occurs.

- Identify and define both the problem and desired solutions through the creation and dissemination of a compelling story that embodies core values and vision and solicits support. Your solution needs to be realistic enough to seem possible but radical enough to really deal with the situation; visionary enough to motivate people to slog through the long fight ahead but based on values traditional enough to seem legitimate; and empowering enough to improve people's ability to shape their own lives but non-threatening enough to allow at least some group of decision-makers to be persuaded to support it.
- Identify, convene, and get commitment from a variety of potential contributors to the advocacy campaign; starting with an inclusive core group with a range of skills and connections – from activists to funders.
- Know your facts; you need at least a rough sense of the implementation challenges – funding, staffing, technical, legal – and ways these could be dealt with. Advocates need to have solid foundations for their proposals so that their ideas cannot be simply ignored on technical grounds.
- Pick good targets and meaningful goals. The policies, programs, and developments you wish to change probably involve multiple players in different levels of different organizations and public or private sectors. The most obvious and

direct target may not be the one you have the most influence over. And what you hope to achieve should have the SMARTIE components: *Specific* (clear and simple), *Measurable* (using transparent methods), *Achievable* (by your group and its allies), *Realistic* (seen as doable by media and others), *Time-limited* (so you aren't stuck in an endless tunnel), *Inclusive* (so that broad alliances are possible), *Equitable* (both the process and result will reduce disparities). Furthermore, it is dangerous to make all of an advocacy campaign's goals things that can only be given to you by others. It is important to establish – and publicize – goals that are under your own control such as number of events and members, submission of laws and court cases for consideration, etc.

- Develop unifying initial strategies for publicizing your grievances, getting your proposal adopted, and monitoring its successful implementation. The core group needs to identify the other groups and interests it needs to win over or neutralize, or whose opposition it needs to overcome. In particular, you must figure out how to appeal to the self-interest of the people and institutions you need to approve and implement your proposals. Of course, all these will evolve as the campaign progresses, and you seldom end up with the same strategy you started with. But it helps to start with some ideas.

- Begin to shape public perception and receptivity. Nearly every advocacy campaign should begin with public education of some kind – letters to the editor, leaflets, visits to key officeholders and agency administrators, home visits, and community meetings. Getting others to accept your framing of the problem is as important for advocacy success as brand positioning and image is for a corporation's product sales.

Helpful Attitudes

Commitment and organizational skills are a vital part of successful advocacy and movement-building. But, in addition, there are a number of other underlying attributes, beyond good luck and timing, that can make or break any effort. Here are some of them:

BUILDING BROAD COALITIONS; DEMANDING WIDE BENEFITS

Inertia rules – things continue as they were until forced to change; nothing moves in a new direction unless it is pushed. Creating change starts, as Margaret Mead is often credited as saying, with a small group. But successful campaigns and long-lasting results require larger, stronger, broader coalitions.

The ideal coalition defines issues and operates in a manner that provides all members with a stake in victory – that works within a "win-win-win" framework. Big structural changes will have big effects on many stakeholders who will inevitably join the opposition if they feel their own well-being could be endangered by the coalition's demands. For example, eliminating fossil fuels in favor of renewable energy affects not only the general public but the workers whose jobs may disappear, not only communities (often low-income or non-white) in which dirty-fuel infrastructure already exist but also the communities in which the new facilities will be located. Some of those stakeholders may have issues that are even more pressing than fossil-fuel pollution – housing, police brutality, job safety, etc. Working through all this requires endless discussion, multiple iterations of demands, and the careful cultivation of personal relationships leading to trust.

MANAGING ARMS-LENGTH ALLIANCES

Partnerships are between groups with deep and broad areas of agreement. They are not quite mergers, as each group maintains its own identity and there may be areas of mild disagreement between them. But, like a marriage, it's a long-term commitment.

Coalitions are among groups that simply agree about a few things, but can have significant differences outside the relatively narrow scope of their demand-focused alliance. It is possible for coalitions to be partnership-like, or for some members of a coalition to be very close to each other while others are more distant. In either case, a coalition is usually shorter-term and less demanding -- to the degree that in some coalitions, each member group is free to pick which of the coalition demands and campaigns it wishes to participate in and to what level of engagement it wishes to contribute.

Still, if coalition members already have a lot of general agreement, holding out for stronger coalition positions is a high-leverage strategy that can move an entire movement in a good direction. More typically, however, the only thing that everyone can agree on is that they oppose something, or on a specific and limited common demand.

The strategic value of a coalition is that it significantly increases the breadth of support for a particular issue, making it harder for decision-makers to ignore your demands. An experienced organizer once told me that "if there aren't parts of your coalition that make you feel uneasy about being associated with them, then the coalition isn't broad enough."

African-Americans and women should never tolerate racist or sexist behavior within a coalition, but that doesn't mean that fighting society's racism or sexism has to be the only or even the primary public focus of every coalition they join. Especially since, exactly because racism and sexism are so deeply ingrained in our society, it is possible to be active around the climate crisis for example in ways that address the disparities in how it has affected different populations. It may be hard for a women's group to join with an anti-abortion church group around a demand for more day care. But it would be harder to lose a chance to win that demand.

The process of social change is full of contradictions and unlikely alliances, partial victories and system-preserving compromises. Being part of a coalition does not mean giving up your own organizational identity; it does mean finding areas of agreement rather than getting stuck in difference. It does not mean abandoning your politics; it does mean remaining aware that even you may have something to learn.

ACKNOWLEDGING OFFICIAL PROCESS; RESPECTING INSIDE ALLIES

Bureaucracy is the opposite of direct democracy. Yet even at its Kafkaesque worst, there is a core of logic to its procedures and schedules. The odds of getting official action improve when you know how to play the system by its own rules – even when they are stacked against you. This doesn't mean that you always follow the rules, but knowing what you are not doing can help cut through the red tape.

Furthermore, although it may be hard to remember when you are pounding on the doors to be let in, in almost every agency or business there are potential allies – people who share some of your vision or values and would love to do more but are constrained by their own organizational context. At best, if properly positioned, they can help make the bureaucracy's "official" response to your demands as positive as possible, creating a better starting point for subsequent negotiations. Staying connected with insiders also helps keep advocates from ending up on the irrelevant sidelines of policymaking. There are a lot of hard-working, dedicated public servants out there – we need to help them succeed.

BEING PATIENT; RESPECTING TIMING

Constant pressure often is the key to success; but it can also turn your effort into ignorable background noise. Sometimes repeated pulses are more effective, allowing you to regroup in between upsurges. Judging when to pause to consolidate what has already been won risks alienating those unwilling or unable to wait for more; but pushing further than is currently possible also risks exhausting and dissipating the campaign. It is always a tough call. You have to monitor progress against the evolving context, deciding when currently maximal success has been reached and needs to be secured.

Change usually comes in irregular waves. Success is most likely when many different forces and trends come together, which is difficult to predict and slow to develop. And even then, things seldom move quickly – until the moment of opportunity arrives and it all seems to happen overnight. (Which is why advocates always have to have their "big ideas" already on the table, vetted and "shovel ready" to be pushed into action on short notice).

It is important to know when to go "all-in" and when to "call," or even to "fold" and wait for the next round. But even in the deadest of times, it is important to find ways to keep the vision alive, find allies, build coalitions, and celebrate the victories we have won no matter how small. Our lives are long. If we wish to remain active for the duration, we need to pace ourselves. It is far too easy to burn out.

In football, Vince Lombardi supposedly said that "winning isn't everything; it's the only thing." But in advocacy, winning is more typically experienced as a series of positive steps rather than a single game-ending score. Still, given how hard and long most campaigns can be, it is vital to claim intermediate victories – encouraging your supporters, maintaining momentum, and providing another opportunity to do public education and media outreach.

Leadership

Good leadership is as much a function of personality as of skills and experience. Leadership can be taught, but not everyone can learn. Still, there are ways to view leadership as having multiple and separable roles that opens it for broader participation. Leadership in representing or connecting to key constituencies. Leadership in helping resolve internal disagreements or creating an inclusively welcoming interpersonal tone. Leadership in speaking to the press or creating an active social media presence. Leadership in organizing events. Leadership in developing strategy – understanding the surrounding context well enough to identify the issues and activities that sit in the sweet spot of being ripe for change, able to attract resources, and within the organization's capabilities. Leadership in donation-soliciting and fund-raising. Administrative leadership: people able to stay on top of the endless paperwork and digital respon-sibilities, financial monitoring, regulatory reporting, database generation, website and mailing list updating, and the countless other tasks needed to keep things going and legal.

But there still is a need for the old-fashioned overall executive leader – someone who can hold the whole thing together. It is sometimes possible for a group of people to develop a truly democratic and egalitarian collective leadership process. But it's a rare and wonderful feat. In fact, even more important than col-lective leadership is the ability of leadership to empower the rest of the organization – to make everyone feel included and useful. My father told me that there are three kinds of leaders: the kind that when it's all done people say, "he did it." The kind where they say "he led us." And the kind where people feel that "we did it together!" In advocacy, as in business and government, excel-lent managers are hard to find and excellent leaders even harder. If you have one, keep her.

Sustainability: Personal And Organizational

I recently attended an advocates' meeting titled "Intergen-erational Discussion." There were about 60 people ranging in age from their late teens to 80, about half non-white, half fe-male, representing various gender self-identities and class back-grounds, and all active community organizers around a variety of issues. The younger attendees, in addition to complaining about generally not being taken seriously by older people in their own organizations, most urgently wanted advice about how to keep going over the long run.

They were worried about finances – the cost of living (and the burden of student debt for those able to go to college) has be-come so much higher in recent years that it is hard to live on what organizers usually make. It is hard to support your children or gain the security of homeownership or even think of eventual retirement. The collapsing social safety net makes the prospect of future illness or job loss scary. But the younger people were even more interested in the emotional aspects of life-long activism. Given how much effort it takes to get anything done, given how lopsided a balance there is between losses and victories, given the personal price activism takes in terms of careers and even family life – how do we do it?

On the personal level, the most profound response was given by long-time African-American community leader and former City Councilor, Chuck Turner, who said that sometimes you have no choice. And then he added that, as a person who had paid a high personal price over his lifetime of activism including imprisonment, if you are fully committed to a vision or mission or set of values and ideals, then the details of your personal ups and downs are not as important. The Movement is what gives your life its context and it carries you along.

Some of the older people, particularly the non-African-Americans, had had more flexibility and choice in their lives. They said that we have to remember that one of the insights of the 1960s was that change comes from within as well as without – it is legitimate and necessary to work on personal change and growth as much as on social reform and justice. We have to accept that we go through our own life stages and need to adjust our activism accordingly. At certain times we can be the spark plug that makes things happen: an _organizer_. At other times, we are an _activist_ who goes to meetings or writes letters when asked by others.

At yet other times, or in different circumstances, we are a _supporter_ contributing money or showing up at demonstrations. And, in many situations, we are simply a _sympathetic bystander_, talking about issues or events in positive terms in conversations with our family and friends. (I remember when my own children were first born. My main form of community involvement was sitting at the back of meetings and falling asleep. It won me approving comments from the older women but, to be honest, didn't move the group agenda forward very much.)

Several people said that keeping on requires the creation of friendship networks and supportive communities – which grow best when we are as good to each other as we try to be to the oppressed and exploited. Others echoed Emma Goldman's slogan that "if you can't dance, it's not my revolution" by saying that activists need to find time for fun and relaxation. Still others said that maintaining our own mental health requires us to occasionally forgive ourselves for our inability to accomplish all we think needs to be done.

We have to avoid feeling responsible for everything everywhere, to ground our global idealism with attention to what's immediately around us. It also requires us to be more understanding about what the nature of an advocacy victory actually is – never total or final; as much about process and small re-arrangements as about dramatic transformations.

Everyone agreed that long-term involvement is built on a willingness to remain open-minded, to keep learning from others and from the world around you what is needed and what can be done and how it can happen. We need to maintain our passion, but manage its expression.

Several people said that it helps to accept the reality of the volunteerism version of the 80/20 rule – that 80% of the work would inevitably be done by 20% of the people (meaning ourselves), although it was always important to encourage the less-active 80% to contribute in some way. At the same time, there was general agreement that developing new leaders and building a team spirit was vital, even if that took time and attention away from campaign work.

It was obvious that there were no "correct" answers. We do what we can with what we have, relying on family and friends and colleagues and ourselves.

Organizations Are Not Forever

Organizations sometimes undercut themselves through excessive concern for self-preservation, in which the health of the organization takes precedence over the growth of a movement or even the success of a reform effort. Taking risks is a necessary part of advocacy. Sometimes it is necessary to stick your neck out, to start a project for which you don't have a funding source, to take on an issue that stretches your resources further than feels comfortable, to jump even if you're not sure where you will land.

Because they rely so heavily on volunteers and pay staff so little, advocacy groups are particularly fragile. If your governing body or staff becomes repeatedly deadlocked, divided between unyielding factions, it may be better to split apart into two groups. Even the presence of an endlessly argumentative person, or someone who simply doesn't fit in with the social dynamics of the group, can be deeply destructive. That person might be adding a vital perspective to your deliberations. But it may also mean that the group is becoming unable to make decisions, to move from discussion to action, and that group processes and events become dysfunctionally stressful rather than productive – and therefore extremely unpleasant. Few volunteers will want to keep wasting their time in that kind of situation, and the organization will slowly (or quickly) fall apart. Better to accept the pain of expulsion than the agony of collapse.

Sometimes, including in the advocacy world, a group has served its purpose, or the context has changed and the group is for some reason unable to adjust strategies to meet the new challenge, or the group has run out of energy through the loss of its leadership or some other reason. Sometimes, when action is impossible, the best strategy is to step back and concentrate on education — on preserving your vision, analysis, and lessons-learned while accepting that the next wave of activism will address the issue in its own way. After dedicating years to an issue and an organization, it is very hard to forgo enough ego and identity to let it go. But it may be time to move on.

5. ADVOCACY AND MOVEMENTS:
Creative Anarchy, Effective Organization

Small acts can make a big difference when there is a background of concern, understanding, and preliminary activism.
NOAM CHOMSKY, POWER SYSTEMS: CONVERSATIONS ON
GLOBAL DEMOCRATIC UPRISINGS AND THE NEW CHALLENGES
TO U.S. EMPIRE

No fundamental social change occurs merely because government acts. It's because civil society, the conscience of a country, begins to rise up and demand - demand - demand change.
PRESIDENT JOE BIDEN

Just because a bad situation exists doesn't mean that positive change will occur. Human history is full of long-lasting injustices and practices destructive to people and the planet. Suffering and mistreatment have never been absent from daily life. Inertia rules human society as much as the physical world; current conditions tend to maintain themselves; those who benefit from a situation use their relative advantages to stay in control, to keep things as they are.

And yet change always comes. Sometimes for the better. Often involving tireless efforts by people inspired by hopes for a better life in this world, or perhaps in their children's. Advocacy is often slow and its effects small; advocates often feel isolated and weak. Activists often wish for a mass movement able to create sufficient political pressure to force the leaders of government or business to take more radical, sweeping, and permanent action. In fact, contributing to the process of creating a mass movement is a secondary but highly desired goal of most advocacy organizing.

Unfortunately, movements do not appear on command. The exact timing of the movement's explosive emergence into public life and the exact combination of events that ignite it – as well as the extent to which it becomes not merely a ripple in the social fabric but a tsunami surging across the land – all this is utterly unpredictable and uncontrollable. Throughout history, peasant revolts, labor strikes, and urban uprisings have started and spread at moments and with a swiftness that always astonishes the attacked rulers. Today, social media has created digital wormholes connecting previously distant people, facilitating mobilizations on a scale and at a speed previously unimaginable.

At its best, a movement is more than a protest, more than an outburst of anger at an intolerable situation, more than an effort to veto a threatening change. At its best, a movement is also a demand for a more positive alternative, often an idealist or even utopian vision that goes beyond single issues into a more holistic, value-based aspiration for better life. Movements are an explosion of human creativity, a manifestation of bottom-up people power.

Movements burst into view as anarchistic, self-mobilized eruptions of people, each participant doing their own thing in ways that reinforce a common theme or effect. Movements flow and grow, seemingly inventing their strategy as they go, while leaders desperately try to organize the energy into particular tactical directions. Movements exemplify the collective self-organization of mutual support that decentralists dream about. To paraphrase Karl Marx, uprisings are as much festival as statement.

Those of us who have participated in mass movements, who have experienced the joy and affirmation of being surrounded by tens of thousands of like-minded people, who have internalized the life-altering realization that nearly everything about human social existence is shaped by human beings and can be changed through collective action – we are the lucky ones! We know that "the personal is political" in ways that have given meaning, satisfaction, and community to our lives.

Those of my generation who were fortunate enough to be involved with the movements of the 1960s and 1970s know that they transformed us personally, professionally, and politically. Civil rights (and the successor liberation) movements, anti-war (and the more radical anti-imperialist) movements, the counter-culture (and its personal liberation) movements, the women's and gay liberation (as well as the subsequent gender identity) movements, the anti-nuclear and deep ecology (as well as the contemporary climate protection) movements – for many of us, participation fostered permanent changes that have shaped the course of our lives ever since.

Harvests Are Sown In Fertile Soils

Movements are not primarily expressions of desperation and despair. The emergence of a mass movement also requires a degree of hope, a belief that change is possible and victory might be within reach. The small victories that good advocacy campaigns create can contribute to this positive attitude.

Still, no matter how much hoped and worked for, mass movements only arise when sufficient tension builds up between the various layers of society, when "internal contradictions" make it impossible for old patterns to continue. Just as the shifting of tectonic plates floating across the earth's mantle creates mountains and seas, earthquakes and volcanoes, movements emerge in response to deep, structural changes in the economy, in technology, in the natural environment, and even in the international balance of power. The changes disrupt old alliances and old assumptions. Things fall apart. People feel their well-being or status threatened. They look for reasons and enemies.

But anxiety and anger are not enough. People must also have the perception that the current governing elites are unable or unwilling to deal with the situation; that those in charge have abandoned their responsibilities and left those below them to fend for themselves; that the bosses are no longer legitimate rulers and no longer need to be obeyed.

This changed perception could be caused by the ruler's military defeat – examples are the mass movements forcing the collapse of the Argentine military dictatorship after its defeat in the Falklands, and the fall of the Greek military after its loss of Cyprus.

Economic tensions could energize regional cultural and political splits that eventually spawns irresolvable conflict. This happened in the US in the mid-1800s when a coalition of western family farmers and northern craftsmen allied with emerging business leaders arose in opposition to the dominance of southern slavery-based plantation entrepreneurs. Or the inherent contradictions of an economic system may push conditions into crisis, the way capitalism repeatedly cycles through booms and busts making possible system-wide power shifts the way the Great Depression led to the New Deal.

Technology may undermine previous systems of social control -- the modern Civil Rights Movement partly emerged because of the post-WWII mechanization of Southern agriculture, which loosened the immobilizing bonds of share-cropper peonage and convict-leasing forced labor, and set the stage for the Great Migration of African-Americans to northern cities.

 Or there may be some natural disaster (or climate change!) that overwhelms the ability of a society to meet people's basic needs for food and water, such as the deadly post-earthquake inaction of the Nicaraguan Somoza dictatorship which opened the door for the Sandinista uprising.

Part of the context for a movement's growth may come from outside. The legalized separation and privileging of whites in the American South – an apartheid system that was the inspiration for South Africa's later version – was enforced by violently repressive actions by both law officers and private citizens. The African-American community fought oppression in subtle ways in every aspect of their daily lives. But they did not have the strength to overthrow the system by themselves. External allies, with greater political and military strength, were needed; some top-down leverage was necessary to pry open the closed Southern way. The signaling of support from the national Democratic Party, no matter how symbolic and half-hearted, was a key turning point for Congressional impact.

When crisis hits, when things fall apart and old patterns no longer function, if the rulers are not able to adapt quickly enough, if they appear to have (as Chinese folklore says) "lost the mantle of heaven," – if key layers break apart -- there is an opportunity for new forces to arise. It is as if an earthquake opens the ground and the underlying lava pours out.

But lava is too thick and sticky an image. Movements are more accurately described as political waves. They aren't permanent or, usually, long lasting. They rise with the energy of unseen winds, sweep on to shore, and then sink into the shifted sand. If the deep-ocean conditions are strong enough, there may be repeated series of waves lasting generations. But like waves, they are time-limited. They reshape the beach and perhaps the land behind it, creating a new environment for the survivors to inhabit. But once their energy is spent, waves disappear.

Preparing The Ground

Although movements seem to appear as if by spontaneous combustion, they simply sputter out unless there has been a slow accumulation of fuel created by the years of quiet resistance and small but brave efforts of large numbers of ordinary people. In 1909, W.E.B. Dubois wrote:

> It is not always the apparent leaders who do the world's work. More often those who sit in high places, whom men see and hear, do but represent or mask public opinion and the social conscience, while down in the blood and dust of battle stoop those who delivered the master-stroke – the makers of the thoughts of men.

(JOHN BROWN, BY W.E.B. DUBOIS)

On top of this, movements take hold and spread because of resources previously positioned in key locations -- years of preparatory work by organizers and funders, trained leaders, ideologists and popularizers of supportive factual and narrative arguments, communication and activist networks at regional and local levels. All this creates people, and groups, with the skills and agency to recognize and respond to an opportunity.

Like a prairie fire, this spreads the sparks to other areas with potential fuel. The wind that turns smoldering unrest into a conflagration fire comes from good leadership with adequate resources – and a lot of luck. The current growth of right-wing politics, for example, was prepared for by several decades of expensive investment in think tanks, student organizations, media, training of people to run in local elections, political contributions, and experimentation with various issues and alliances to see which were able to attract an audience.

Progressives are beginning to do the same. Says Deepak Bhargave in *Of Ducks and Democracy*, (The Forge website, 12/8/20):
[The most successful are] long-term organizing efforts, built year by year and [election] cycle by cycle, and they relied on recruiting and training thousands of volunteer leaders whose names will never be tweeted or celebrated in the New York Times op-ed page. Stacey Abrams is a genius, but what makes her so is not only her prodigious individual talent but all the other leaders she helped to gather, develop, and train, and the organizations she built for the long haul.

Even over-ripe conditions are not enough to make change happen. There must be a trigger. The events that spark an uprising occur randomly at unpredictable moments – the same thing that passes for depressingly "normal" at one point suddenly is explosive at anther. For all the money spent by right-wing billionaires and churches, the ultra-conservative religious fringe and the Alt-Right neo-fascists were minor players until 9/11 raised people's feelings of insecurity and made many vulnerable to fear-based appeals for stability against "others."

But, if conditions are ripe, it is sometimes possible for strategic-ally smart protest groups to provoke and escalate an "ordinary" situation into a launching pad for large-scale mobilizations. The lunch-counter sit-ins, the Freedom Rides, the voter registration marches were all designed to create un-ignorable events, create a trigger. No matter how rotten, the tree in the forest does not fall until it is pushed. And nothing pushes history like a movement.

Contextual Constraints, Movement Limitations

Successful mass movements combine contextual change, elite dysfunction, and popular engagement. They require the right combination of hope, anger, leaders, supporters, resources, and political space. They emerge out of their context.

The layers of context are related, with the larger (global or na-tional) setting limits on the possibilities of the smaller (regional or local or personal). So, global climate patterns and inter-national power relations set the parameters for national eco-nomic development and domestic political dynamics, which set the parameters for local prosperity and family well-being, and so on down to our individual lives – the aspects of our person-ality and interests that are able to develop or left to shrivel. It's a dynamic system, there are forces moving both downward and upward, inward and outward. While each layer moves according to its own dynamics, its limits are set by the adjoining layers.

Movements often transform the lives of the people most in-volved and may push society forward for a while. But for a movement to affect policy and institutions during the often-long intervals between uprisings, during the quiet times when people just try to live within the limits of what exists, it must use the power of its peaks to create and energize sustainable activ-ists and organizations – advocates and groups.

Social Change Starts Invisibly

Movements are visible and massive. But they are only

part of a much longer and often invisible social change process. In 1986, long-time organizer Bill Moyer – co-founder of the Movement for a New Society and the Social Movement Empowerment Project – rewrote his seminal analysis: *History is a Weapon: The Movement Action Plan.* It was originally inspired by the feeling of defeat that spread among members of the anti-nuclear Clamshell Alliance after their occupation of a proposed nuclear power plant site in New Hampshire didn't stop the project. Moyer wanted to explain that it was exactly the opposite: a huge victory. They'd turned nuclear energy into a topic of national debate and inspired the creation of hundreds of similar grassroots groups across the country.

Moyer described social change as a process that goes through eight stages, only a couple of which involve demonstrations or provoke headlines. In the first stage, *"Normal Times,"* problems are generally taken as unquestioned givens by the media and general public; activists focus on researching what is actually going on. During the second stage, *"Proving Institutional Failure,"* activists use established procedures to raise objections and prove the inadequacy of normal channels; however, in general, business and politics continue as usual.

"Ripening Conditions," the third stage, sees the emergence of small advocacy groups focused on the issue and the beginning of direct action; while public awareness is growing the majority still support the status quo and protesters' demands are ignored.

In stage four, *"Take Off,"* "trigger events" lead to large demonstrations and widespread awareness; mainstream groups are pushed by established interests to oppose or discredit the now visible movement. The wave of activism crests and ebbs in the fifth stage, *"Perceived Failure,"* as entrenched interests dig in and activists are exhausted.

But if sufficient energy can be maintained or major institutional failures occur, *"Majority Public Support,"* the sixth stage, can be achieved – although threatened interests become aggressive in their counterattacks, sponsorship of fake facts and "independent" groups, and use of the legal system to raise public doubts, misdirect regulatory efforts, and repress their opponents. *"Success,"* stage seven, is quickly followed by *"Continuing the Struggle"* in stage eight, as policy-change victories need to be followed up by implementation.

Movement Building: Self- And Social Transformation

For much of American history, the "mother of movements" was that against the institutional racism of slavery, Jim Crow segregation, mass incarceration, and the incorporation of racial discrimination into every aspect of our national culture. White ownership of black-skinned people was the original sin of the United States, built into its core structure and culture; the most vicious of its democratic failures. The Civil Rights Movement of the 1960s had deep, historic roots going back to colonial times. And it also modeled much of what we know about movement-building.

The early Student Nonviolent Coordinating Committee (SNCC), active in the early 1960s, was committed to the belief that the only way to raise an entire house is to lift the basement. Their participatory vision of democracy, and the violent denigration of Southern blacks in every detail of daily life, led to a deeply grassroots strategy of building a movement from the bottom up. This reinforced SNCC's powerful understanding that movement-building involved personal as well as societal growth and change – by participants and organizers alike.

The power of this approach comes from the dignity with which it treats previously overlooked people, its uncompromising democratic egalitarianism, and the resulting emergence of previously silent voices as part of a process of unleashing, as SNCC organizers Robert (Bob) Moses and Charles E. Cobb Jr. describe in *Radical Equations*, "the vast resources in communities that seemed impoverished and paralyzed at first glance." SNCC saw itself and the people it worked with as part of a centuries-long movement of Afro-Americans fighting for individual freedom, group dignity, and collective empowerment.

SNCC's approach combined respectful listening to local people, particularly those not currently represented by established organizations, with patient support for their development of the skills and confidence needed to lead their own struggles. It emphasized a commitment to indigenous rather than staff leadership, participatory democracy in decision-making, and mistrust of most existing organizations because of their internal hierarchies and their compromises with the status quo.

SNCC recognized the need for a coordinating or even an organizing role: Bob Moses, a leader of the 1964 Mississippi Freedom Summer voter registration campaign, felt that organizers should find the people who are heading in the right direction and organize everyone else to go with them while creating "space" that "cultivated and protected these voices." In *Radical Equations* he notes,

> "what we learned in Mississippi [is] that it is getting people at the bottom to make demands, on themselves first, then on the system, that leads to some of the most important changes....We [organizers] didn't create the civil rights movement...what we did was create a network that helped sustain and advance the movement."

STRENGTH FROM BELOW

This style of organizing works best when there is a broad (even if latent) agreement within a community about common grievances that community organizing helps surface, get articulated, and be taken up by local people. It works even better when there is a long history, as there was in the African-American community, of struggle against outside oppression. And it only works if the organizers have a patient, long-term perspective.

The strength of such a movement is that it can embrace both an explicitly political demand such as voting rights and a broader vision such as personal and cultural liberation. In "This Non-Violent Stuff'll Get You Killed", Charles Cobb Jr., a former SNCC Field Organizer, distinguishes between the "Civil Rights movement to secure equal rights under the law....and the Freedom Movement whose goal[s also include] a liberated sense of self and human capacity." As Bernice Reagon, founder of "Sweet Honey in the Rock" says, the Movement "gave me the power to challenge any line that limits me."

However, as people trying to follow this approach repeatedly learn, there often is a tension between the slow and localized process of base-building and leadership development versus the need to win visible victories; between focusing on what most immediately matters to local people versus the pressure of the large-scale issues that initially brought organizers into the community; between the commitment to bottom-up leadership versus the need to cut deals with outside, high-level decision-makers; between the avoidance of hierarchal leadership versus the pressure of the celebrity-creating media to personalize stories.

Organizers often feel other pressures. A sense of overwhelming personal responsibility for stopping our nation's repeated violence against Black people or stopping its murderous invasion of Vietnam – feeling a desperate need to create immediate change – weighed heavily on early SNCC organizers and contributed to their original campaigns being overshadowed by less patient and less nonviolent strategies.

BEYOND LOCAL LIMITS
SNCC's power came from purely bottom-up strategies. Lyndon Johnson's manipulation of Congress to force passage of the transformative 1964 Civil Rights Act was top-down politics. And there are effective strategies in-between. Dr. M. L. King Jr., working through the Southern Christian Leadership Conference (SCLC), believed that local work would get lost unless its visibility was elevated in some way. In order to connect local efforts

with federal-level pressure on Congressional negotiations, he used his celebrity to draw national media attention to an issue as leverage for raising the priority of protesters' demands among national leaders and organizations who, in many cases, would have rather not gotten involved.

For example, President Lyndon Johnson was sympathetic to the Civil Rights Movement's demands, but his priority was ending poverty, and he didn't believe he had enough political support to push both issues at the same time. But, as dramatically shown in the movie Selma, the brutal police attack on the March to Montgomery that Dr. King flew in to lead sparked national headlines and outrage, raising Civil Rights to a top political priority and helping push Congress through the drafting, submission, and passage of the historic 1965 Voting Rights Act.

Capturing The Moving Spotlight

Dr. King's SCLC created weeks-long or months-long campaigns that escalated an issue and often provoked opponents to misstep or over-react. This allowed SCLC to occupy the moral high ground and to appeal to national leaders to force local reactionaries to implement existing national values and laws. But this only works if the celebrity of the leaders and the outrageousness of the opponents can hold media attention long enough for public outrage to percolate and the demanded action to occur. When the cameras go away, progress stops.

King understood that national media, public concern, and national politicians all have very short attention spans, so success required having a very specific demand as well as a general vision of larger values and desired change. While local activists felt that the Albany Movement changed their lives, King saw it as a policy-level failure: "The mistake I made there was to protest against segregation generally rather than against a single and distinct facet of it. Our protest was so vague we got nothing."

Critics described SCLC's approach as a "fly in, fly out" program and warned that "if the media makes you it can also destroy you" (something that J. Edgar Hoover tried to accomplish with his repeated release of information about King's personal life). They complained that King's style perpetuated the African-American community's traditional hierarchal relationship between clergy and congregation. They also pointed out that if the campaign fails it is the local people who are left to absorb the consequences – from increased repression to murder. However, there is no doubt that King energized the Civil Rights Movement, inspired millions of people to take action, and leveraged political change on the national level. And it's also true that increasing its visibility among decision-makers – usually through media coverage – is a central need for every movement.

RADICAL INCLUSION

The Civil Rights Movement exhibited another theme often central to mass movements. It was a fight to secure rights that its participants were theoretically already supposed to have. At least in the political rights phase of the movement against explicit racial segregation and voting exclusion, African-Americans were fighting to exercise rights supposedly already granted by the US Constitution. They were fighting for inclusion into American society and government rather than its overthrow, a demand that however radical in the context of Southern reality was "simply" demanding that national norms be applied in a non-conforming section of the country. It was the "name and shame" framing of Southern exceptionalism that made SCLC's media-mediated appeal to national public opinion an effective strategy for pressuring national leaders.

SCLC recognized their dependence on the long-term work of local organizers and grassroots-based organizations such as SNCC as well as the willingness of ordinary people to take dangerous actions. The defining characteristic of both the SNCC version of community organizing and the SCLC version of high-visibility campaigning is that they saw themselves as part of a larger, centuries-long movement-building process fighting for personal growth, culturally and religiously sanctioned social values, and long-overdue civil rights.

Movement Life Spans

Ironically, a movement's strengths are sometimes its undoing. For example, one common trigger for a movement's emergence is that a large number of people feel significantly threatened in a similar but avoidable way. The anti-Vietnam War student movement got a great deal of its energy from the prospect of coming home in a body bag. The anti-nuclear testing movement grew from a fear of annihilation. When the draft was canceled, and the test-ban treaty signed – both representing significant victories -- each movement collapsed, even though the underlying issues remained.

In addition, movements are hard to sustain. Unless a movement coalesces into more organized and focused effort, it will eventually run out of steam, as did the amazing Occupy Wall Street movement against growing financial sector–caused inequality in late 2011.

The complications of actually implementing its vision can also dissipate a movement's energy. Movements often start out seeking radical transformations. But short of the collapse of old institutions, the exile of former elites, and the often-widespread suffering that occurs during a revolutionary break with the past, the best-case end result of mass movements is usually reform. As they grind through the inertia of what is and the complexities of creating something new, as they seek to expand their support beyond their radicalized base, as they try to consolidate what they've won even as their opponents regroup for counterattacks, movements usually end up discarding their more radical overtones and focus on securing specific improvements or on the inclusion of formerly excluded groups into a higher level of the mainstream.

During a movement's rise and ebb, the old establishment may

have fractured, but each faction will have found new allies within the insurgent movement whose needs could be satisfied in ways that allow at least some of the old elite to retain their position and privileges, and that allow society's institutions to continue creating hierarchies, even if some newcomers are now allowed in. Of course, the bigger the movement and the weaker the control of elites opposing it, the more significant the reforms that can be won.

This is part of what happened to the militant industrial labor unions of the 1930s, whose radical initial visions held a promise of a better America for all, but were forced into narrower "wage and hour" boundaries under the repressive weight of Cold War attacks period.

The Women's Liberation Movement suffered from this narrowness as well. Radical feminists originally envisioned the total transformation of sexual relationships, family dynamics, as well as the structure and culture of the business world. It's true that many fathers now spend more time with their kids than they used to, and day care is no longer routinely described as an excuse for maternal negligence. But the movement's biggest structural impact was to force business to open up the job market to individual women, not to raise the minimum wage or stop maximizing profits through wasteful consumerism. The Gay Liberation Movement once sought to redefine sexuality; but its successful fight for same-sex marriage only came after re-orienting itself to demand inclusion into the conservatizing institution of legal family bonds. The Civil Rights Movement has not ended racism, but it has made it legally difficult to explicitly exclude people because of their skin color – and led to a man of color becoming president even during the lifetime of people who remember lynchings.

CREATING SPACE
Even if they don't accomplish most of what they set out to do, even if they fade away, movements create important political

space and open the door for subsequent upheavals. The Occupy Movement, for example, quickly grew and then died. However, in the process it changed our national consciousness and sparked a revival of progressive activism across a broad range of issues. It was the Occupiers' denunciation of the power of the 1% that made Bernie Sanders' presidential campaign against inequality possible. It was their re-opening of space for activism that the Black Lives Matter movement moved into. It was their denunciation of earth-destroying profiteering that provided a platform for the rebirth of a climate protection movement.

Movements also directly spawn others. For most of the past 70 years it was the Civil Rights Movement, confronting the core racial contradiction of our democracy, that mothered others, starting with the Black Power and Black Liberation movements. The first anti-poverty activists, the organizers who pioneered what would become the Great Society's War on Poverty, were students who brought their Southern experiences back to Northern cities. Those who returned to campus began the anti-Vietnam War (and anti-imperialist) movements. The Women's Liberation Movement spun off from those, and then birthed Gay Liberation, which laid the base for the explosion of activism around AIDS, which led to the astonishingly successful Marriage Equality campaigns and then the gender-identity issue.

Candles In The Dark

History is not predetermined. People are creative, able to break through at least some of the contextual layers confining them. And, in most cases, the energy and inspiration required to make those breakthroughs possible, that position us to seize transformative opportunities, come from mass movements. Mass movements set the stage for change, not only for the macro-level restructurings but for the smaller reforms as well.

However, for all their importance, mass movements are not enough. They set the stage but do not speak the lines. Voice comes from the presence of strong and sustainable advocacy organizations capable of harnessing the movement's energy for specific victories through effective campaigns for institutional reform.

And most issues will never generate mass movements. The coincidence of underlying interests, demographic latency, and triggering incidents for a movement is an unusual occurrence. As a result, most of the time advocates channel their feelings into non-dramatic, issue-oriented work. But to have more than individual significance, this requires organization. Being part of an organization magnifies the impact of individual effort, provides a focus for volunteers and supporters, and encourages collective input into decision-making.

My father, a teacher, used to say that it's better to light one candle than curse the darkness. In those long-ago arguments, I used to counter that society's need for fundamental improvement required systemic changes so deep and so threatening to established interests that accomplishing it would be impossible without radical action.

We were both right, of course, although (as usual) his slogan was easier to remember. We do need visionary goals. And achieving them will require the kinds of radical change that is only possible at moments of crisis, when systems are failing and the establishment's hold on power is weak. But being able to take advantage of those moments requires years of small-scale work. And this requires advocacy as well as movement-building.

We have to do what we can. Rabbi Hillel's insight is as true today as it was 2,000 years ago: "If I am not for myself, who will be for me? If I am not for others, what am I? And if not now, when?"

6. CREATING MEMBERS, CHANGING BEHAVIORS:

Building Sticky Organizations and pattern-changing policies

If you want to go quickly, go alone. If you want to go far, go together.
AFRICAN PROVERB

There is strength in numbers, but organizing those numbers is one of the great challenges.
JOHN C. MATHER

Groups require members. Advocacy groups need people to not only see the group's ideas and demands as legitimate but to also believe them to be winnable. Even better is when people become willing to act: to personally do something individually or with others that will help turn the proposals into reality -- to become supporters, participants, activists, organizers, leaders. Members. And through their activity help attract more members and supporters – including the needed extended informal network of funders, informed media people, and friendly decision-makers – who all become part of a self-reinforcing virtuous cycle of progress. An organization's most important asset is its activist core group.

As with advocacy in general, individual motivation generally starts with protest, or at least a feeling that "this is not right; this must stop!" People go up a ladder of engagement through the "AIDA" sequence – *awareness, incentive, decision,* and *action.* Once a person gets involved, they are more likely to stick around, to join and remain a member of an advocacy group, if their anger can turn into hope, if that hope is confirmed by some level of success, and if success leads to a belief that collective action can prevent that kind of problem from happening again. In addition, the more that participation provides opportunities for self-growth and meaningful personal connections, the more people continue to participate.

Facts And Stories

Individual recruitment starts with public outreach, both to educate people about the facts and to change the public perspective or frame of understanding about your issue. Public education, getting out the facts, is often a necessary starting point for advocates because the public usually knows so little about an issue. Or we've been deceived: we now know that the world's major oil companies knew for decades that burning fossil fuels would cause environmental disaster; they even began building their sea-drilling platforms higher in preparation for rising sea levels. But they also spent hundreds of millions of dollars financing bogus science and phony "astro-turf" citizen groups to create action-preventing uncertainty.

Even if status-quo defenders are not spouting lies, it is likely that people's understanding is distorted by a fog of widely believed falsehoods based on old assumptions, sensationalist media coverage, and TV thrillers. A large percentage of our population does not know that the majority of people receiving public support are white, not black. Crime is primarily committed by citizens, not immigrants. Households with guns are more dangerous than those who rely on the police for protection. Facts ground you in reality; their absence leaves you unanchored in a make-believe world, subject to emotional manipulation through the repetition of cultural stereotypes and prejudices. Facts are the bedrock on which effective strategies rest.

Of course, some people are so committed to their beliefs that facts cannot penetrate, regardless of the persuasiveness of countering arguments. Trump cultists have denied the reality of a COVID pandemic even as they die. And we are all susceptible to a long list of cognitive, judgement, and logic errors.

In today's world of unchecked information inundation, the Enlightenment belief that truth emerges from rational discourse based on repeated testing – the scientific method – has become suspect. It has become culturally acceptable to deny the possibility of objectivity or the validity of an evidence-based consensus. Instead, pop culture upholds the legitimacy of different kinds of "truth" – from spiritual to emotional, from social to personal. And, in fact, there is much evidence that our reasoning process of logical thought rests on a foundation of emotions, that we work our way through the many options of a logic tree to reach a decision based on how the outcome feels. So, even for the more open minded, facts alone are often not enough to create belief in their veracity.

NARRATIVE LEVERAGE

What can be transformative, able to change someone's frame of understanding and underlying perspective so that they interpret events in a new way, is the emotional power of the narrative that surrounds the facts. Narratives that turn facts into a story that gives listeners a version of events that makes new sense, with a moral message that helps give relevance and meaning to the person's own life.

Our exposure to a new way of seeing can be either empathetic or experiential. It can come from hearing a story that puts everything into a new light. Or it can come from contact with someone else's reality. Or living in a new place. Or starting a new job. The shifting of one's mental and social context creates a jolt that not only helps loosen the hold of old ideas and assumptions, but also opens the possibility of reconsideration and reorientation.

Person-to-person outreach creates relationships that are the most effective medium for this type of communication. Recent studies suggest that occasional voters are over two times more likely to go to the polls if talked to by someone at their front door than if they receive a phone call reminder. To make the changed behavior permanent requires a surrounding community of reinforcing believers and confirming experiences of follow-up success.

Becoming Sticky: Personal Change And Growth

In the long run, it is success that makes organizations "sticky" and members loyal. Everyone loves a winner! Failure to solve problems makes people leave. While some people may dedicate their lives to fighting a noble but lost cause, advocacy organizations and their campaigns will only maintain broad participation if they seem to have the power to at least partially achieve their members' political and personal needs.

For most people, the political is intertwined with the personal. Advocacy campaigns must be meaningful and measurable – both in terms of their societal impact and of participant's experience. A new vision of societal possibility, of potential political change, also connects to a new vision of themselves – shifting from passivity to activism, from an identity as victim to actor, from cynicism to hope. This needs to be concretized through a well-supported, incremental path from newbie to core group and leadership. People seldom start as full-blown organizers. More likely, we start as empathetic _observers_. We may then move to interested _supporter_, to low-key _participant_, to consistent _activist_, to facilitating _organizer_ of others, and perhaps to strategic _leadership_. Not everyone climbs the entire ladder. Not everyone should – there are valuable contributions to make at every step.

Related to this is the opportunity to personally grow by learning new skills, making new relationships, or gaining entry to a wider world. Friendship and community also increase stickiness – they are what nourishes sustained engagement. In my tenant union days, we hosted monthly parties and weekly soccer games as well as frequent potluck dinners. The brilliance of the "social unionism" of the early labor movement was that it addressed the full range of people's needs and gave entire families avenues for learning and growth. And people will stay involved so long as the group continues to feel useful in enough of these ways; so long as there is positive social interaction. Even if the campaign dies out, you'll have each other.

INCLUSION AND EXCLUSION

Most advocates are volunteers. They are freely choosing to come to a particular event, attend a meeting, help with tasks, tell others about the group, contribute, or anything else. Not surprisingly, they are most likely to stop coming if they feel that the effort is doomed to failure, especially if they expect to have to pay some personal price for participation. But long before it gets to that point, the presence of obnoxious and obstructionist others is likely to drive them away. It is the worst kind of "liberalism" for advocacy groups to allow someone to dominate meetings, treat others disrespectfully, disrupt group efforts, or otherwise be a social problem.

More often, however, people are turned off by events and meetings at which they feel marginalized, excluded, or disrespected by the language, procedures, cultural assumptions, and social dynamics. Racism, sexism, homophobia – these are not merely societal problems but also organization killers. There are many first steps to take:

- language translation (for non-English speakers),
- avoidance of jargon,
- assigning a "buddy" to every first-time attendee responsible for getting together outside of the meeting,
- setting up a new member welcoming committee to run introductory discussions,
- including both educational and action components in every meeting in addition to the inevitable administrative updates,
- putting time limits on speakers,
- and being clear about decision-making procedures.

Some techniques can feel artificial but can break through difficult problems: requiring that every male or English-language or long-time-member speaker be followed by a women, immigrant, or newcomer.

But some of the problem is subtle, especially in terms of class and racial dynamics. As a society, we are still learning how to talk about and address racism. Our history of slavery and institutional discrimination still shapes every aspect of our society. But class-based cultural differences can also be problematic. A public housing tenant-union activist I once worked with finally quit the city-wide leadership group because she felt she was losing touch with her working-class neighbors and family. She felt she was getting too caught up in the world of the college-educated organizers, lawyers, and bureaucrats she was working with on a daily basis. The more that the campaign is based in the population whose interests are being represented, the less these tensions are likely to emerge, but they're unlikely to disappear.

Changing Behaviors That Change Minds

Members are those who join. But even after taking that signifying step of commitment, changing behavior can be difficult. Even more difficult is figuring out how to change the public's behavior. "If everyone only acted better," is a common complaint. We typically think that changing people's ideas, educating them, will change their behaviors. But it may work the other way – that changing the context is what changes behaviors, and it is the changed behavior in a reinforcing environment that causes them to change their minds. People who work in fully racially integrated firms tend to believe fewer racial stereotypes. The death of so many families' cousins from AIDS forced many deniers to acknowledge that homosexuals were people. It is the presence of a gun in a house that escalates the feeling of being under siege.

Policy is the tool we use to change behavior-shaping context. However, it needs to be done subtlety, indirectly, changing the least obvious aspect of the larger environment. Putting a fee on the inclusion of carbon in a product leads consumers to change buying patterns in response to new patterns of price differentials. However, using policy to directly change behaviors can come across as incredibly patronizing if not coercive. The pushback against New York Mayor Michael Bloomberg's proposed ban on the sale of super-sized soda containers forced its cancellation – "how dare that billionaire try to tell me what to drink!" Covid-pandemic mandates to wear masks and prohibit large gatherings have been furiously and openly violated by churches, businesses, and most Republican Governors.

This is one reason for the popularity of an "empowerment" approach to this strategy – indirectly affecting behavior through policies and programs supposed to give people the tools and support for making changes in their own lives. The popularity of the idea at least partly stems from its redirection of action from eliminating the institutional barriers to people's advancement to personal responsibility for getting ahead.

COLLECTIVE EMPOWERMENT

From an advocacy perspective, the best empowerment programs are designed in ways that create stepping stones for additional advancement for individuals while creating vehicles for collectively addressing larger systemic problems. At a minimum, it is vital that individual solutions happen in a collective manner; that they bring people together to experience the commonality of their problem, understand it as a systemic rather than individual failing, and facilitate collaborative action for both mutual aid and program reform. The goal is not merely solving individual problems or allowing individual advancement, but shifting the balance of power.

These goals are complicated and difficult to embody in policies and programs. They must provide short-term meaningful and visible improvements in participants' lives even before the longer struggles to address the underlying causes of their problems begins to succeed.

Not surprisingly, these types of programs are often criticized as asking too much of a single program that usually has barely enough resources and political support to survive – a often valid complaint. Getting such policies and programs adopted, and then properly implemented, requires persistent work backed up by strong political pressure, and the strategic ability to build the full agenda through incremental steps over an extended period of time.

Sometimes, the campaign demanding the creation of such programs is as politically valuable as the program itself. Radicals typically believe that asking for something that large numbers of people understand as legitimate and needed, but that the current structure of society is unable to provide, reveals institutional limitations and gains support for more fundamental change. Success at each stage of program development can empower the campaign, prove the concept, and bring in additional allies.

Revolutionary Reforms

Advocacy campaigns need to demand four overlapping types of actions: symbolic, initiatory, significant, and transformational. Symbolic actions are designed to make a public statement, to send the message that things are changing. Speeches, banners, signs, celebrations, and other symbolic actions don't, by themselves change very much. But they do help to prepare people for change to come. Initiatory actions are similar – visible, easy, non-controversial, and quickly accomplished, they make it clear that change is starting, even if the effect of these actions is minimal or short-lived. Painted bike lanes quick wear off, but they let everyone know that road restructuring will come.

Significant actions begin addressing the deeper symptoms and causes of a problem, reforming programs, policies, and behaviors. If those changes also begin to reverse the historical pattern of multi-generational inequality, if they begin to change the long-term power relationships that maintain various hierarchies, then they move into the realm of <u>transformation</u>.

In his book, *Strategy for Labor*, Andre Gorz calls these transformative, power-shifting programs "revolutionary reforms."
He describes them as changes that improve people's material
well-being while also democratizing power relationships and
decision-making, and thus altering the terms of political debate. He calls for a strategy of creating organizations that counter institutional power – tenant unions, food and housing coops, community councils, citizen review panels for police, and
others.

The hope implicit in a revolutionary reform strategy is not only
the standard empowerment goal of helping people get rid of
hope-killing fatalism. It is also to give them the skills and collective power to overcome the "learned helplessness" that makes
them unwilling to challenge the powerful because "it never
works" and "there is no alternative."

The success of revolutionary reform movements changes
people's consciousness and lays the foundation for future advancement. Even if unsuccessful, asking for something that
large numbers of people believe is both needed and legitimate,
but that the current structure of society is unable to provide,
is radicalizing and increases support for more fundamental
change. It is also true that the radical reforms of the past can
turn into new niches of well-being, turning former rebels into
defenders of the new status quo. But the next round of struggle
will, at least, be starting from a more structurally democratic
place.

These campaigns are winnable, especially when the current
ruling groups and their allies have been discredited and deeply
split by inability to solve an economic crisis, or by losing a war,
or suffering some other extraordinary setback. In such circumstances, one wing of the Establishment might reach out to a bur-
geoning mass movement, offering radical reforms in exchange

for support. This may not lead to the overthrow of the entire system, but it can create significantly better lives for the majority of people.

Advocates have to continually try to change the minds and behaviors of potential recruits, supporters, and allies. But it is important to remember the limitations of such efforts. The goal is not to convince everyone – just enough people for the campaign to continue, grow, and win enough victories to make the effort worthwhile. It is a sobering reality. But better to celebrate what you have done than to condemn yourself for not doing it all.

SECTION III:

THE POLITICAL FUNCTIONS OF ADVOCACY

The prize for movements is not particular victories, but changing what people perceive as obvious and natural and normal and what's coming next.

BILL MCKIBBEN, FOUNDER: 350

7. GAINING INFLUENCE:
The Three Phases of Advocacy – Protest, Pushing, Partnership

8. CHANGING INSTITUTIONS:
The Systemic Functions of Advocacy – Mobilizing Political Will, Ensuring Agency Capacity, Securing Permanence

7. GAINING INFLUENCE:
The Three Phases of Advocacy – Protest, Pushing, Partnership

If there is no struggle, there is no progress. Those who profess to favor freedom, and yet depreciate agitation, are men who want crops without plowing up the ground. They want rain without thunder and lightning. They want the ocean without the awful roar of its many waters. This struggle may be a moral one; or it may be a physical one; or it may be both moral and physical; but it must be a struggle.

FREDERICK DOUGLAS

[Anger is a powerful impetus for social change when] focused with precision [and able to distinguish between potential] allies with whom we have grave differences, and...genuine enemies.

AUDRE LORDE

If we ran the world, we wouldn't need to advocate for anything. We'd just do it, or order it done. But, almost by definition, the need to advocate for something implies an outsider status, without direct control over decisions. True: individual advocates are sometimes prestigious or influential. Their requests are listened to, carry weight, and adopted by decision-makers. But much more commonly, advocates – and those they are advocating with or for – start from a position of relative weakness, perhaps even a degree of invisibility. They are forced to advocate because they currently lack the power to make decisions or impose their will on others. Advocacy starts a step away from power, based on the need to gain influence in a decision-making process being carried out by others.

Gaining influence requires taking a series of steps towards power: changing the current situation to increase individual or group benefits or to cause institutional change. Sometimes, the goal is to get an agency or program to simply follow its existing rules or enabling legislation. Sometimes, advocates want new policies, procedures, staffing, or evaluations. In either case, advocacy starts from the outside and works inwards.

True: outside advocates sometimes have an inside "champion" – someone who agrees with your goals and has the power to make it happen. Sometimes, often because of the advocacy campaign, the political environment allows that inside person to smoothly implement the desired change. Often, however, despite the insider's willingness, the political context makes it impossible to proceed. During the New Deal, President Franklin Roosevelt supposedly told advocates, "All right, you've convinced me. Now force me to do it." But, in the more typical situation, where the relevant decision-makers are opposed to, or insufficiently supportive of, your demands, you've got to pressure them. And that requires acquiring influence.

There are many kinds of influence. With the possible exception of one-on-one cajoling on the basis of personal relationships, securing any of them usually requires going through at least three strategic phases: Protesting against what you don't want; Pushing for what you do want; and Partnering with the implementing agency to make sure it's done right. The phases overlap, combine, and repeat with the objective of moving the target agency, institutional practices, or overall system through the desired changes. This is what advocates build organizations for and seek power to accomplish.

(Institutional change -- the transformation of an organization and its operations, has its own series of phases that are discussed in the next chapter: creating political will both outside and inside the organization; ensuring that the agency staff has the technical skills needed to carry out the mission; maintaining public support for the changes during the almost inevitably rocky initial stages; and making the reforms as permanent as possible by integrating them into regular budgets and job descriptions.)

Protest: Demanding Attention, Exercising A Veto

The strategic goal of protest is to stop the normal unfolding of the status quo; to force key decision-makers to notice you and acknowledge the existence of your objections; to disrupt "business as usual" in order to open political space and begin occupying it. There is a danger of disrupting things so much that the people being advocated for are at risk of losing more of what they precariously already have than what they will potentially gain. There is also the danger that the powers-that-be get so scared that they counterattack – perhaps violently – in ways that the advocates are not prepared to deal with. However, usually, as one state official told me, "politicians respond to noise; keep making noise."

In addition to capturing attention, the job of protest is to change the framework within which an issue is discussed. The Occupy Movement's "99% versus 1%" slogans didn't directly cause any policy or legislative changes, but their insistent visibility did make inequality a central part of the national political dialogue.

In the most serious situations, when the problem is deeply rooted in the core systemic dynamics of society, and if the protests have become large enough, the goal might escalate to creating enough disruption to undermine public confidence in the ability of society's rulers to keep basic institutions functioning. Raising the stakes this high almost always causes counterattacks, but can also force worried elites to take more positive action in an effort to dampen the anti-establishment anger. It was this fear of societal dissolution, a fear that things were getting out of control and that too many types of hierarchies were coming under attack, that persuaded some national leaders to turn against the US war on Vietnam.

Still, in the beginning, when you are starting from relative weakness, you have to find some way to get the attention of people beyond your initial core group – both those you wish to mobilize and those you wish to influence. You need to become visible: letter writing, showing up at events, demonstrations, media coverage, endorsement of your issue or group by prominent people. The trick is to seem to be speaking for a bigger-than-you-already-have constituency while presenting yourself in ways that help turn that appearance into reality. Probably less than 1% of Americans actually participated in a 1960s Civil Rights or anti-war demonstration, but their issues were framed and acted upon in a way that resonated with broader swaths of the larger population.

Of course, the classic people power tactic is to bring noticeable numbers of angry people out onto the streets or into a meeting. This doesn't take a lot of people. If you're really lucky, the situation feels a bit tense, with a subliminal threat that things might get out of control, provoking your opponents to over-react and do or say something stupid – which is one way to gain enough friendly media attention to get your issue officially noticed. As protest grows it becomes less dependent on the miss-steps of others. Writing in *Nature Human Behavior* (2019), political process researchers Erica Chenoweth and Margherita Belgioioso point out that social movements starting off with "relatively modest popular support" can significantly increase their impact by increasing the frequency of disruptive activity through boycotts, strikes, and other forms of high-participation actions – a strategy that "was more dependent on their own resources, organization, and stamina than on the response of the opponent."

THE POWER OF "NO"
Protest is a powerful and vital advocacy tool. Most change starts with protest of some kind: an expression of anger against racism or police violence or a war you want to stop. If it can tap into the deeper feelings of frustration or fury that many people carry within them because of family or societal misuse, it can rapidly escalate – as did the Trumpian takeover of the Republican Party. Being "anti-something" is a simple concept to grasp; people in other neighborhoods or around the country can quickly copy illustrative actions and start local efforts, drawing on their own creativity and local networks. Decentralized protests are an excellent example of anarchist organizing, such as the Occupy Movement, the preceding anti-World Trade

Organization demonstrations, and the more recent "Black Lives Matter" activities. Whether decentralized or coordinated, some advocacy campaigns are conducted entirely within the protest stage and still achieve significant results.

Because of protest's limited "anti-something" basis, protests are able to (at least temporarily) bring together broad coalitions of people with very different ideas of what they want to see done once the bad things end. The anti-Vietnam War movement included people who thought it was being poorly executed but supported US intervention elsewhere, people who opposed US imperialism generally, pacifists who opposed all war, and people who simply didn't want themselves or their family members to get hurt. The anti-abortion movement includes people opposed to late-term terminations, to all abortions, to day-after pills, to birth control, and to women's equality in general.

Protest is powerful because it does not have to be majoritarian. Erica Chenoweth, in *Why Civil Resistance Works*, writes that sustained protest or non-cooperation by only 3.5% of a population is enough to force political elites to make major shifts. However, even if not majoritarian, numbers count.

To move from a small-group activity to a mass movement whose general goal has broad, even if mostly passive, support among the general public, protest needs four attributes: disruption, virtue, legitimacy, and escalation. Disruption is what forces society to notice the problems and injustices that the status quo takes for granted; it is the only effective leverage available to have-not outsiders, as Francis Fox Piven and Richard Cloward long ago pointed out in *Regulating The Poor*. The willingness of protesters to endure personal sacrifices – financial loss, blacklisting, imprisonment, hunger, beatings – gives them moral standing, making it harder to depict them as merely self-serving miscreants. Being seen as personally virtuous strengthens protesters' argument that it is their institutional opponents who are the bad guys in the story.

In order to gain broad public support, protesters also need to be seen as legitimate – framing their demands and actions as an expression of the surrounding society's professed values, cultural trends, and political history. While the general population usually dislikes and initially opposes disruption, they are often ultimately willing to bear its annoyances if they can be made to feel they "should" approve of the underlying values and general goals of the movement – and if the protesters' tactics are seen as neither violent or disrespectful of people, religion, or various social norms. Chenoweth's analysis of movements around the world also found that non-violent movements were typically larger and led to political change 53% of the time compared to 26% for violent protests. (This is a key reason that non-violence is strategically important even if the protesters are not pacifists.) And finally, to have societal impact, protest needs to escalate to the point that the combination of disruption and widening approval forces elites into a "dilemma choice" situation – they can either give in to the demands or counter-attack – but things have gotten sufficiently out of their control that the amount of force needed to repress the movement risks dangerously offending the mainstream. And then, if good fortune holds, the protesters win.

THE MODEL
The archetypical protest-only campaign was the fight against the Lower Manhattan Crosstown Expressway in the early 1960s led by urban visionary Jane Jacobs. Against all odds, Jacobs' neighborhood coalition stopped what was generally considered a done deal to build a highway connecting New Jersey with Long Island.

First, they reframed the issue to focus on a small but essential detail of the highway plan. While they did question the highway proponent's traffic numbers, rather than directly deal with the problem of cross-town congestion, they focused on preserving the local neighborhood as a safe place for families. Their slogans, images, and actions all described the horror of destroying the iconic Washington Square Park, a famous and much-loved public landmark. Similarly, by keeping the focus on the particularities of Washington Square, Jacobs didn't allow the debate to be diverted into the merits of her radical critique of post-WWII urban planning. It was a fight over immediate local realities rather than ideology.

Keeping the focus narrow also allowed the protesters to build an increasingly broad coalition. They gave presentations to every possible group. They secured "save the park" statements from prominent business and religious leaders and demanded similar pledges from every politician running for office. Jacobs and her group followed up their reframing with relentless media outreach. They were endlessly visible – sending letters to newspapers, calling editors, packing city meetings, and staging brilliantly theatrical events that captured media attention. Energizing all this work was the protesters' ability and willingness to upset the apple cart – to disrupt meetings, hold public demonstrations, embarrass officials, and to use every available legal technicality no matter how tangential to hold up official plans. And officials' repeated over-reaction, rudeness, arrogance, and use of police against the protesters further undermined their credibility and created waves of public sympathy for the demonstrators.

The anti-Expressway protesters always acted as if their demands were the only acceptable moral position. They were right; period. The Expressway people were wrong; period. There was no room for compromise: fewer lanes, less taking of homes, burying the highway under the park – all were rejected as violations of the core principle of no destruction of the neighborhood and the Square. Absolute rejection, turning a protest into an all-or-nothing fight, is a high stakes strategy – if you don't win you can lose everything: the highway might have been built. But in the right circumstances it can be very powerful, almost like religious fundamentalism. And this strategy is most likely to work when the campaign, like the anti-Expressway fight, is entirely a "stop it" protest. It wasn't demanding an alternative approach to dealing with through traffic. It wasn't demanding new investment in community development. It was simply focused on stopping the highway – and purely "anti" or "stop it" fights don't have to worry about painting themselves into corners from which no positive program can emerge. As it turned out, the highway was stopped and a national movement was born.

THE LIMITS OF PROTEST

Protest is an outsider's game, the exercising of the only veto available to those with little formal power. Protesters may have a positive alternative in mind, but as a protest movement they have very little control over what those in power do in response to their efforts. The impossibility of controlling the response to your protest by decision-makers can put advocates in a difficult spot.

Boston's African-American community had been protesting for several decades against the terrible education their children were getting. Letters. Presentations. Demonstrations. Sit-ins. Boycotts. Freedom Schools. The key issue was the unequal treatment their children were receiving even within a school system that, by the 1960s and 70s, was so thoroughly focused on patronage that few students of any color were getting much of an education. The key demand was that the schools be improved: busing was not on anyone's list.

However, years of protests went unanswered. African-American parents ended up left with a court case based on the refusal of the city's School Committee to obey state non-discrimination laws. The inescapable guilty verdict meant that educational issues would be dealt with primarily as a desegregation problem, and that the solution would be decided upon by the judge rather than the community. The protesters wanted better schools; what they got was cross-town busing. But once that solution was offered most of the black community felt they had no choice other than to rally around it for fear that otherwise they'd get nothing. The anti-busing backlash was violent, bringing racism to the surface, and further locking African-Americans into defense of something they hadn't particularly wanted.

Of course, if you don't like the response to your protests you can continue to protest – which can be very effective so long as your numbers, energy, and disruptive visibility remain high. But because protest is often even more disruptive to the protesters' daily lives as it is to those who they are trying to influence, it is hard to maintain over the long haul. The high drama needed to capture media and political attention, needed to keep an issue's visibility and priority high, requires large-scale mobilization and can provoke oppressive responses from established power. Winter comes. Bills are due. Other responsibilities call. People get arrested. The Occupiers eventually go home.

No matter how dedicated the participants are, large-scale protests are hard to sustain against entrenched, institutional opponents capable of waiting out a difficult stretch. I've been involved in fights against University expansion where the institution's 50-year planning horizon simply outlasted our community efforts to influence their use of local land. Chinese protesters in Tiananmen Square in 1989 found that the country's authoritarian state was quite capable of waiting until momentum waned and then crushing the remnants of the democracy demonstrations.

For these reasons, sustained protest typically takes the form of embedded and non-dramatic daily resistance, primarily by those most trapped within a social problem. Daily resistance is expressed in small, often private actions – although they are often noticed by other people suffering from the same problem. The "invisible work" of family and community maintenance despite worsened conditions, often by women, is one form. So is subtle non-compliance with offending social norms or orders from above. So is non-standard cultural expression and surreptitious mutual aid. So is deliberately poor work habits, songs, and social ties. These are all foundations for solidarity. If sufficiently widespread, and if the quiet resistance is strategic enough to make governing difficult or profits difficult, they might have an effect on elite decisions. This is how non-violent resistance to oppression can begin. However, in most circumstances, by itself, this subterranean opposition has limited impact on the source of the problem.

Over time, living with oppression and repression pushes anger and resentment inward like a coiled spring. It can create enormous internal stress in people and communities, sometimes leading to self-destructive or anti-social behaviors. When triggered, the latent fury can explode. But, like private resistance, unfocused angry outbursts are not enough at either the personal or community levels. Anger, abuse, and riots do not make things better. Anger becomes an effective protest only when it becomes visible, collective, and more painful to the larger society than to those expressing it.

THE MILITANCY MOTOR
Society is often quite willing to ignore problems and injustices, no matter how grievous. Disruptive action, sometimes requiring escalating levels of militancy, can force society to pay attention. Even if the protesters themselves are ignored, their presence opens political space for less disruptive others. Massachusetts Congressman Barney Frank often said that one of his most valuable allies were the groups that made his demands seem moderate. Opening up a "left flank" in a campaign creates more political space for moderates to lean left. This is true both in terms of the analysis and demands being presented as well as the tactics being employed.

But militancy in tactics is often confused with radicalism in content. Groups can raise a ruckus for very moderate goals. Very extreme demands can be presented in very quiet ways. The best combination of the two depends on what you're trying to accomplish and the setting in which your action takes place.

Sending a "wake up call" to decision-makers, letting them know that not everyone is OK with the status quo can be done with a simple letter or a few speakers at a public event. You can mount a show of strength by packing a meeting with button-wearing silent people. Forcing recalcitrant officials to let you speak, or stopping a meeting from taking place, requires disruption, which usually takes a combination of non-violent civil disobedience and noisy tumult. The setting can be an event organized by people whose agreement or support you hope to gain, or by a "neutral" group whose goodwill you do not want to forsake – both situations requiring you to remain non-disruptive. Or you could be at a meeting with hostile government or business groups whose interests (and past actions) make them an enemy, deserving of a full-on confrontation.

Regardless of the setting or the tone, the trick is to come across as reasonable to potential allies and unyielding to opponents. Sometimes tactical sequencing works: starting with polite explanations explaining your position, then escalating into noise and action nearer the end. Sometimes, the silent presence of large numbers or even the visibility of a few people representing those hurt by a situation is more effective than "shut-it-down" boisterousness. It is important to think through what can be gained beyond an opportunity to simply express your own anger.

The greater the level of disruptive militancy the greater the need for group discipline, a clear – and publicly announced – set of principles and guidelines for action: non-violence (rather than an undefined "diversity of tactics" relating to destruction of property or physical attacks), respect for non-involved people (or even opponents as individuals) caught up in the action; safe roles for those not wishing to risk arrest through civil disobedience, etc.

THE ACTION FACTION

Groups and movements almost always have an "action faction" –
people opposed to "analysis paralysis" and "death by discussion"
– who deeply feel that the issue is too important to be delayed,
that extreme militancy is both morally required and politically
necessary. The action-now strategy does get people moving and
often forces attention on important issues. Militance can push
groups "from protest to resistance" by "putting your body on
the line" through refusal to conform, civil disobedience, or even
physical confrontations – as did Vietnam War draft resisters,
anti-logging tree sitters, today's "pipe closers," and others.

SLIDING INTO DANGER

Unfortunately, there is often a dangerous confusion surrounding militancy and violence – two very distinct categories of
action. The essential edge of chaos around a protest event or
movement creates space that can be filled by people with anger
and issues far removed from the original cause, and whose
statements or actions may end up discrediting the entire effort.
While there are circumstances that justify being quietly prepared for physical self-defense, pro-active or public preparation
for violence is almost always a poor strategy, often legitimizing overwhelming counterattack. During the Civil Rights Movement, rural southern African-Americans, who often owned
guns as part of that region's hunting culture, would sometimes
let it be quietly known that they were "around" churches holding voting rights meetings. However, the meetings themselves
never called for violence – exactly the opposite: people who
could not commit themselves to non-violence were asked to stay
away from public demonstrations. As people from Gandhi to M.
L. King Jr. to David Dellinger have shown, revolutionary non-
violence can be as forceful a tool for social change as the barrel of
a gun.

Anger at injustice or a feeling of personal responsibility for
society's mistreatment of others are powerful motivations for
positive action. However, it can be a slippery slope. Letting your-

self feel too much of others' pain can drive you crazy, especially if you believe it could be stopped and that you are partially responsible for making that happen.   Given a particular personality type and the dynamics of small, isolated, or beleaguered groups (both political and religious) the stress can lead to such poor analyses of reality, such self-justifying moral outrage, that ideological perspectives over-rule understanding of how change occurs, and violence seems to make sense.   The Weatherman spin-off of the anti-Vietnam War movement believed the killing would only stop if they "brought the war home" by attacks within the USA. Earth First saboteurs felt the globe-threatening destruction of our forests and environment was threatening nature itself. Anti-abortion bombers feel that participating doctors are murderers. The feeling of totally righteous fury drove people in each group to movement-undermining violence.

It's also vital to distinguish between protesting for a cause and what I call Apocalyptic Disruption, in which creating chaos is itself the goal – based on the belief that society has become fundamentally corrupt or that the country as a whole is the enemy. This can be religiously motivated: some fundamentalists believe that evil has taken over the world and their God will only return when the false temples are destroyed. Radical Islamicists get the most press, but there are similar tendencies in Christian, Hindu, and Jewish fringes as well. It can have political motivation: for example, Minuteman vigilantes who believe the US government and most of our society have been taken over by a conspiracy of Communists, UN agents, and Jews; and the Weather Underground Organization of the anti-Vietnam War movement who believed they had to "bring the war home" in order to stop it. Or it can be motivated by emotional implosion: when someone or a group catastrophically feels their world is collapsing and they want to take everyone else down with them – as expressed in several of the mass-murder/suicide horrors in Jonestown and, more recently, Sandy Hook, Virginia Tech, Columbine, and too many others. People stuck in these narrow perspectives are a danger to themselves, the movements they try to ride, and society as a whole.

When the situation is sufficiently intolerable and change is intractably refused, it is understandable to feel that an explosion is needed to break the logjam. However, even if it doesn't turn violent, the demand for ever-escalating militance can lead activism into a dead end of self-isolating ineffectiveness. In fact, frequently, the push towards extreme militance involving physical or property harm is eventually revealed as the work of police agents setting up a group for discrediting violence and subsequent arrest – a tactic we now know the FBI successfully and murderously used against anti-Vietnam and Black Power groups in the COINTELPRO program. Whether or not one believes in non-violence as a moral principle or simply see it as a pragmatic tactical and strategic orientation, it is a powerful and effective method of avoiding being set up for defeat by your enemies.

Pushing: Positive Visions, Specific Ideas

Protest can force decision-makers to pay attention to you and stop what you don't want. It is, however, a negative force – it doesn't get you what you do want. Even worse, the exhaustion of prolonged effort and the inability to control the response to your protest can leave advocates in the difficult spot of having to live with, sometimes even defend, inadequate "solutions" that have been imposed on you.

To get the desired policies, programs, and processes requires pushing a positive agenda. There are some issues that can't even be successfully protested without also addressing positive alternatives. For example, given the intimate incorporation of fossil fuels into energy and products, fighting climate change is almost unimaginable without describing other ways to meet (or change) our basic needs, production processes.

Part of getting decision-makers and the institutions they control to move from denial and resistance to a positive response, is having clear proposals about what you want them to do -- how to stop bad things from continuing to happen, how to redress the negative results of past malfunctions, how to restructure tor re-orientate the process. Often, this requires having, or drawing upon, a significant amount of technical expertise about the problem, potential solutions, and desired measurable outcomes. Knowing what you are talking about often has the added benefit of gaining some respect (however grudgingly given) of the professional staff in the target agency, which makes them more likely to take your suggestions seriously – laying a useful foundation for the time that they will be assigned responsibility for implementation.

The downside, of course, is that you are also taking on the risk of having your proposals criticized, of getting "lost in the weeds," and of losing some of the energy of your protest and the support of some part of your coalition. But remaining silent about what you want, or simply refusing to put details on the table, makes it very hard to create the future you want.

Moving from protest to pushing is not always possible. The opposition may be strong enough to keep you stuck in getting noticed. But when possible, it is an important path forward.

CULTIVATING INSIDE ALLIES

It is possible for pushing, like protesting, to be entirely an "outside" effort. You can keep bringing your proposals to the agency's doorstep and demanding their adoption. Sometimes a move from the outside using well-framed media coverage that suddenly makes an issue visible is all that is needed to prompt a positive response from relevant decision-makers. These communication-focused tactics are most likely to succeed if the needed action is relatively non-controversial, if doing it won't threaten any established group's status or power, and if there is little organized or vocal opposition. It helps if your organization already has the legitimacy of a successful track record or is supported by already powerful people. But if you're just an ordinary citizen or new group, tossing ideas over a wall hoping someone picks them up isn't the most effective strategy. It's much more effective to have inside allies who echo your arguments and push your ideas from within.

Sometimes, frustrated insiders secretly reach out to you, glad that someone is finally pushing for the improvements they have been unsuccessfully advocating from within. More likely, you get quiet clues at meetings or via intermediaries that there is a faction of the staff who are also dissatisfied with the current state of affairs – although their solutions may differ from those you prefer, their dissatisfaction helps create space for your own. However, your ability to leverage each other's efforts partly depends on the tone of the protests that got you all to the same table. Were you angry at the situation or nasty to the staff? Assertive about your demands or contemptuous of the staff's deficiencies? Outraged at the dehumanizing outcomes, or insulting to those whose job descriptions forced them to be part of it? As much for self-serving reasons as for its likelihood of being true, it's important to project a public stance that it's not the agency staff that you're protesting but the bad policies and dehumanizing procedures they're forced to carry out, and their negative impact upon people and society.

LOBBYING

The "pushing" phase of advocacy can be seen as a kind of lobbying. Lobbying has a negative connotation – a form of influence-peddling that is inherently corrupt. But even though it is frequently used by the powerful as a backdoor method of exercising their dominance, there is nothing inherently immoral about lobbying. Lobbying is simply talking to decision-makers. It is the process of providing your input into policy formation and program design. It's a key way that public needs and desires can be turned into government decisions or revised behavior by businesses. Therefore, it's an essential part of advocacy – you convert your "demands" into concrete "asks" and proposals you want elected officials, agency staff, or leaders of other types of organizations to respond to.

Lobbyists don't present themselves as the enemy of the decision-makers they are trying to influence. Exactly the opposite: they come as friends, sometimes bearing gifts. Typically, lobbying is an insider's game for people with something to exchange – from expertise (lobbyists often know much more about a particular issue than legislative staffers), to perks (politicians are always needing ways to help constituents or supporters, and sometimes don't mind getting something for themselves as well), to money (until we have a decent system of public financing for electoral campaigns, simply knowing that a lobby group might contribute to your opponent's campaign creates pressure on an elected official).

Advocates need to play this game in a different way. They, too, can offer decision-makers expert input and ideas. More importantly, without violating laws prohibiting non-profits from promoting one candidate over another, as part of their allowable "public education" function they can offer public recognition, praising politicians and other officials for doing something good. They can offer a platform for making announcements and presentations as well as mentions in newsletters. These are all crucial components of a politician's election campaign and of appointed officials' continued ability to serve. While it's important for advocates to avoid becoming (or being seen as) totally within a particular politician's or political party's camp, it is just as important to take electoral politics seriously and find ways to participate in the push for good policies and people.

Getting access to decision-makers is the necessary door into lobbying. The rich and powerful usually get their requests for an audience quickly attended to. A world of social networks and personal connections based on race and class creates extremely unequal access. But, in every type of society, personal-connection-based access to others exists. The best advocates can do is take advantage of their own connections when they can. And, in fact, the longer (and more successfully) an advocate has been involved with an issue, the greater the likelihood that she will have developed personal relationships with top decision-makers and the more she can (and should) use those connections to further the effort.

Furthermore, although one-on-one private conversations are very useful, lobbying doesn't have to be done behind closed doors. "Citizen Lobbies" bring large numbers of people to the state house to ask their representatives to vote for or against something – an action that played a key role in Boston neighborhoods' success in stopping highway expansion in the 1960s and 70s.

MODELING YOUR VISION

Being clear about what you want can be done in many ways. Words are powerful, sometimes examples are even better. One approach is "Tactical Urbanism"—the unofficial implementation of desired changes done on a modest scale but surrounded by as much publicity as possible. The goal is to create an inspirational ripple effect. As an advocacy tool, the interventions are often unauthorized guerilla theater. Bicycle advocates in several cities have responded to car- or truck-caused fatalities by surreptitiously painting bike lanes on traffic-heavy streets. A Seattle neighborhood took it upon themselves to paint a mural on the pavement in the middle of their intersection to both beautify the area and encourage car drivers to slow down. (It works!)

Often, the official response is to remove or condemn the action. Sometimes, inside allies use the opportunity to embrace the idea and scale it up. In Seattle, after opposing the unauthorized intersection murals, city government swung around and created a program allowing other neighborhoods to apply to be given supplies (and suggested designs) for self-organizing a block party to do the same thing. In New York the expanding "Play Street" program diverts the desire to illegally (and dangerously) open fire hydrants on hot days in areas with few parks or pools.

"Park(ing) Day" demonstrations started in San Francisco as a grassroots action in defiance of city rules. The idea was to temporarily transform an on-road car-storage space into a people-attracting green space and use this street theater to prompt public discussion about what else could be done with all that pavement currently dedicated to cars. But some traffic departments, including Cambridge and Boston, have since embraced the idea, even giving groups a one-day exemption from having to feed the meter in their repurposed spot.

Partnership: Working With The Enemy

In some ways, the most confusing part of advocacy is the need to change from Protest and Pushing to Partnership, from criticizing decision-makers and agency staff to finding ways to have constructive conversations about how you can help them succeed – or even to look good when they aren't fully succeeding!

It's a difficult transition: Weren't they the people you just spent so long fighting against? Isn't it the agency's job to actually do the work, and do it well? Isn't it your role as an advocate to monitor their every step and loudly complain when the agency staff (inevitably) mess things up? All good points. And yet – at some point it's necessary to balance the benefits of continued protest and pushing against the possibility of losing everything due to renewed attack, perhaps energized by legitimate fury at implementation problems, from those who oppose the entire change.

If the agency is still fundamentally opposed to implementing the new policy, then continued pressure from the outside is appropriate. After all, that pressure is what led to the policy or program to happen in the first place. And, even if things are going well, an awareness among decision-makers that you could, once again, go on the offensive if the agreed-upon changes are not implemented is an important source of the pressure they need to feel to carry things through.

However, what if key leaders and staff in the agency are willing to implement the changes, but there is continued skepticism or even opposition from other parts of the agency, from other agencies, from various politicians, the media, or even segments of the public? Continuing to publicly denounce the agency might be politically counterproductive, even fatal. You need to maintain pressure for high-quality implementation without playing into the hands of those who wish to keep your proposals from happening at all.

GUIDING IMPLEMENTATION
Similarly, what if there is general support for the change and a willing agency leadership, but the assigned agency's staff lacks the expertise or resources needed to successfully carry it out? It is not wise to let them flounder, risking de-legitimization and loss of public support. One option is to find non-local contractors with the needed expertise, and demand that key elements of the work be subcontracted to them. (This also creates a way to get around the barriers of "Master Contracts" that end up forcing cities to only use a small number of pre-qualified, well connected, and often very conservative firms.) This allows advocates to remain outside the agency, retaining their ability to independently monitor progress and push for more.

Another option is to jump in and get yourself involved in the complexities of implementation. Implementation requires an endless series of daily decisions by people deep within the agency bureaucracy who ultimately shape the reality of the program. Advocates sometimes have more knowledge of best practices and relevant expertise than current staff. It might be very valuable to find ways to participate as much as possible in discussions that shape the details of policy and program formation to make sure that the essence of your goals is not lost in translation. Can existing staff be retrained, or do new people need to be hired? Can current vendors and consultants do the job, or should outsiders be brought in? How must existing organizational systems and procedures be revised? Influencing these kinds of operational realities requires having influence inside the organization, at internal meetings and at work reviews.

However, unless you have more political power than advocates usually do, anyone seen as an enemy of the agency will not be invited to participate in those talks and, if invited, will not have their suggestions taken seriously. Your allies within the agency, the people who you need to become internal champions, will have to keep their distance. To have influence requires being considered "part of the family" – a very different category than an enemy storming the gates.

To gain entry to this interior discussion, advocates have to become partners, with enough access and credibility to know what's really going on and enough respect and clout to be listened to when they make suggestions. This doesn't mean that you don't continue to publicly push for as good a policy or program and results as possible. It does mean that the tone of your public work needs to change from condemnation to encouragement and an offer to help. However, a fine line needs to be walked between pushing for better policies, funding, and staffing versus denouncing the agency and its staff as reprehensible failures.

At the extreme, sometimes the partnership turns into a merger when a campaign ends up with the advocates getting hired to work in, or even to lead, the implementing agency – with all the advantages and challenges that change of role creates. The most obvious downside: no longer being able to exert the outside pressure that got things moving in the first place.

INSIDE-OUTSIDE PARTNERSHIP

Insiders, whether high-seniority or newly appointed, are key to institutional change. Working from within – as appointed leaders, professionals, managers, or other staff – provides experience, expertise, and legitimacy (as well as a more secure salary). People whose careers have moved along professional or managerial paths have a vital role as change agents, either on their own or in support of external advocates whose presence can make pushing for internal change more acceptable.

Creating inside-outside partnerships can be complicated, an un-gainly and perhaps risky dance. And it may not even be possible during the initial protest stages of an advocacy campaign, which usually start with an adversarial tone exactly because an agency or business is doing something wrong. But even at these times, internal people can help open doors for negotiation by insisting that "they've got a point; maybe we can lower the temperature by talking."

Insiders who agree that the problems advocates are describing are real and unacceptable, who might even believe that changes the advocates are promoting are reasonable or at least worth considering, have enormous leverage. Insiders might be able to provide important information, perhaps through circuitous channels. In some circumstances they might even be willing to speak out and validate the protesters' claims. Even if they never go public, once the campaign moves into pushing – negoti-ating, for specific policy, programmatic, or operational changes – having a knowledgeable and supportive internal person con-tributing to the discussion can make the process much more productive. And when it comes to implementation, the presence of committed leadership is vital.

RE-AFFIRMING PUBLIC SUPPORT
Whether working from the outside or having moved in, some degree of partnership will be needed to fight off the likely coun-ter-attack. It is almost inevitable that whatever new policy or program that gets implemented will need some testing, adjust-ments, and revisions. The people in favor of change, who are unhappy with or hurt by the old way of doing things, are most likely to be vocal before the change happens. Once the battle for adoption has been won, they tend to drift back into their normal non-public lives. On the other hand, people whose interests or convenience were better served by the former situation are more likely to start yelling once the status quo shifts. And the num-

ber and visibility of things that inevitably go wrong in a new activity amplify and legitimize their "I-never-agreed-to-this" anger. It is advocates' responsibility to cover the implementing agency's rear, to not leave them out on a political limb – to prevent backlash, or at least to outshout it.

This is as much a battle over the way the implementing agency perceives public opinion as over the public's opinion itself. Waffling officials always wanting to bend with the latest political wind will be influenced by whatever side gets its story into the media first. The first couple of exposures set the tone and are particularly influential in shaping decision-makers' subsequent discussions. Making it clear to the people in charge that the public not only loves the changes but wants more is the advocates' job. It uses many of the same organizing and media outreach strategies previously used for protests, but now arguing in the opposite direction. Now advocates have the more difficult job of explaining what has been accomplished rather than denouncing inaction, to praise rather than protest – while still pushing for improvements in the inevitably less than perfect reality.

The need to make public approval visible is especially important in the public sector. Electoral politics is usually a risk-averse business. The last thing a politician or his senior staff wants is public disapproval of something that can be associated with him. If a decision-maker or elected official has the courage to try something new, to follow advocates' suggestion, then it's the responsibility of the advocates to find ways to generate a positive public perception.

In many cases, a relatively small number of people will have direct personal interaction with the new thing. So public opinion is largely shaped by reportage and comments in the mass (and social) media. It is the responsibility of advocates to prepare a serious marketing campaign extolling the new program, policy, infrastructure, or other change. Happy customers and users should be identified and prepped. A dog-and-pony show should visit all the major media outlets. Pictures, videos, press releases, blog posts, and tweets should be distributed. However, advocates need to avoid mindless cheerleading. The tone should begin with praise, mention needed fine-tuning, and end with a call for even more.

Maintaining positive public perception is also vital for successful program implementation, particularly for behavior-affecting policies. The ban on indoor smoking was only sustainable because of widespread approval, even among most smokers who had become convinced that the habit was not only bad for themselves but also for those around them. There would not have been enough police in the world to enforce the new rules if smokers had refused to comply.

"FRENEMIES"
Partnership is the transition from publicly criticizing decision-makers and agency staff to finding ways to have constructive conversations about how you can help them with successful implementation. Advocates don't have to "marry" the agency; but they need, at the least, to enter a "pushy partnership" or even a "frenemy" relationship.

One approach is the "report card" strategy. By pulling together a broad coalition, a set of rubrics can be developed to evaluate the level of achievement – which can serve as both a list of demands for continued improvement in a city's or agency's efforts and a hook for media outreach and public education. If possible, the agency's leadership is given a chance to look over the criteria and then the evaluative results before they are made public – to correct anything they think is inaccurate, to begin fixing things they might have overlooked, and to prepare answers for the problems that remain. Along with the report card, the coalition also releases a "progress report" that both praises what has been accomplished – with understanding of the challenges the agency is facing – and makes suggestions for what more needs to be done.

In a partnership situation, if additional protest is needed, some-times it is helpful to let the target know what is coming. A key part of a partnership should be a promise of no surprises – "we may not always agree, and we may have public fights, but if you keep us informed of upcoming decisions, we will not embarrass you with surprise attacks." Of course, in a deeply adversarial situation tipping an opponent off about your next move would be a mistake. But if you have a relationship with a politician or the head of an agency, warning them about your plans to issue a public criticism helps keep communication channels open, builds trust, and may lead to a quick solution – for which you can claim credit. Advocates are likely to gain more than they risk by privately telling decision-makers that "we are going to go public with this, but we wanted to let you know beforehand in case you want to first talk with us about dealing with it. However, if an acceptable solution can't be found within [a short time], we will move forward with our plans."

At its best, these discussions lead to closer and more respectful relationships between advocates and program practitioners, al-lowing more informal and ongoing interactions about relatively deep levels of daily work. In international negotiations the slo-gan is "trust but verify."

SAYING THANKS
But even if advocates remain at arms-length distance, it is hugely helpful if they find as many appropriate occasions as possible to appreciate the agency and its staff. I have never dealt with a public agency whose staff didn't at some point say, "get-ting what you want from us would be a lot easier if you occasion-ally noticed and publicly praised the good things we do." Public employees, especially, are seldom told "thank you" by anyone; doing so, even privately, can make a huge difference.

A Forest From The Trees

Progress begins at a discouraging scale and speed. The chal-lenge is not the original number of participants or the original lack of response, but in the need to work through the overlapping phases of the advocacy process – protest, pushing, partnership. Doing that successfully is what will increase the support for, and the receptiveness to, the campaign over time. And, to paraphrase the saying about planting trees, while the best time to have started was years ago, the second-best time is right now.

Victories are often tenuous, with opponents just waiting for a chance to undermine or even eliminate what has been accomplished. Faced with such an onslaught, there is a need to defend what's been won even if it's incomplete or poorly implemented. Being a cheerleader for something you know is less than great is difficult, but – no matter with how many misgivings – it is sometimes necessary to preserve a chance for future progress. At the same time, preserving and promoting the vision of what real progress would look like is vital in order to avoid getting blamed for the program's shortcomings.

And we have to always remember that, no matter how good the program we've reformed or created, at some point advocacy must begin again to protest the problems that past success didn't solve or, perhaps, even created.

8. INSTITUTIONAL CHANGE:

The Systemic Functions of Advocacy – Mobilizing Political Will, Ensuring Agency Capacity, Securing Permanence

A social movement that only moves people is merely a revolt. A movement that changes both people and institutions is a revolution.

MARTIN LUTHER KING JR. WHY WE CAN'T WAIT

Revolution comes; not the expected one, but another, always another.

MARIO PRAZ

Advocacy is the progression of values into vision and strategies into action. But action, by itself, just creates wind. The purpose of the action phases of advocacy – gaining influence through protest, pushing, partnership (discussed in the previous chapter) – is to gain the power to create positive social change. This chapter examines the changes inside programs and institutions that advocates need to use that power to accomplish.

Advocacy's most significant political goal is institutional change; changes inside an organization – in its operational rules, cultural assumptions, processes, programs, power relationships, desired results, and secondary impacts. Advocacy's role in large-scale progressive change is a long march through the institutions, slowly and indirectly building towards long-term systemic change – reform of the re-enforcing effect of multiple institutions over time on entire populations. Change through advocacy is an incremental and uneven process. Directly and holistically transforming entire society-wide systems usually requires extremely large-scale mass movements, whose appearance and success is neither often nor assured. Advocacy is slower, smaller, but hopefully steadier effort.

Whether the target is the government or a business or something else, advocates seeking change have to not only get the change adopted by someone other than themselves, but they then have to ensure that the adopter embraces the vision, does a good job implementing the change, and then integrates the new way of doing things into its mission, budgets, staffing, evaluation systems, and work plans. As if that's not enough, advocates also have to find ways to prevent opponents from returning later to reverse the changes.

Advocates gain influence by pushing from the outside. But institutional change requires both external and internal work. The first step towards institutional change, the major goal of the protest and pushing influence-seeking phases, is to *Mobilize Political Will* among those with the power to make the changes you want – elected and appointed policymakers, agency executives, program managers. At the very least, you want them to not block your efforts; at best, you want them to become champions of the change. However, advocates' nightmare is that they win their demands and then the agency or organization in charge of implementation bungles things so badly that the entire idea is discredited. It can take years to recover from this kind of disaster. So, the second step, a major goal of the pushing and partnership phases, is to *Ensure Agency Capacity*, which again requires using both inside and outside strategies.

Of course, because anything new is a disruption to what currently exists, someone will inevitably complain. And their complaints will have some credence because anything new is likely to have start-up problems (remember the Obamacare website?). So, once the new policy or program is rolling out, it is vital to retain public support. Agency and program leaders need to be honest about the problems. They need to bring all stakeholders into the implementation process discussion. This also requires parallel, inside and outside effort. In addition to this internal activity, outside advocates need to repeat the public relations and mobilization aspects of the protest phase, while building on the new legitimacy and media access gained through victory.

Finally, advocates and internal champions have to fight for the *Institutionalization* of their victory. The goal is to secure the *permanence* of the new policy or program or processes by embedding them within the organization's mission, budget, work plans, and staff evaluation systems. Every organization, program, and system has its particular history. This means that changing things in meaningful ways requires a deep, institution-level transformation of the values embedded in its operations and the professional cultures of its staff. This includes hiring practices, public/client interactions, and internal social dynamics. This is far beyond the personality-based manipulations of "office politics." It is a sophisticated process of transformational reforms that fundamentally re-orients the agency and its impacts.

REPRESENTATION

A theme of many contemporary political campaigns is the need for greater inclusion of previously marginalized groups in the employment and program benefits enjoyed by the surrounding society, and for the group members' recognition as legitimate, contributing members of that society. A common component of these campaigns is a demand for representation in decision-making processes and bodies, a demand that expresses the groups' growing self-awareness and collective identity, often around issues of race, sex/gender, age/youth, class, and more.

Representation is motivating and important to excluded groups. It is exciting and validating to see "people like me" in office, in the media, in positions of wealth and influence – or even just on the streets. It is a source of group pride, affirms their presence as "normal" members of society, and symbolically makes them part of the mainstream. The hunger for even symbolic inclusion is so strong that it is one of the most effective rallying cries for mobilizing under-represented groups behind campaigns to elect new leaders. I remember sitting in my living room with a group of friends, African-American veterans of the Civil Rights Movement, the night that Barak Obama was elected to the presidency. They – we – were all crying.

Often, the immediate effect of representational demands is to elevate an individual to a more visible and powerful position. While this may be the first step in a larger reform process, by itself the presence of a symbolic person in high position does not change the realities of daily life for anyone else. The goal is using this "camel's nose under the tent door" opening to further democratize access to decision-making and institutional impact. Otherwise, the victory remains symbolic and temporary. Obama's election did not end racism; in fact, it provided a target for the largest resurgence of racist politics since the post-WWII anti-black riots.

Still, representation is powerful. Improved visibility – whether in political, business, or media – can have a significant effect on the represented group's sense of themselves and of their opportunities. To a lesser and more long-term extent, it might change society's overall culture and sense of what is acceptable. But if the new political possibilities are not realized, and if the benefits of inclusion do not extend to the majority of the group, society as a whole does not radically change.

Mobilizing Political Will

The first requirement for institutional change is political will. The will to act can be imposed from above and within, when higher levels of government, businesses, or other organizations demand change from subordinates. It can come from outside, from public pressure, either through pressure on those higher levels of power or directly on managers of the target organization or program. Or it can even come from the "rising to the occasion" of leaders within the target organization.

The goal is to get relevant decision-makers to "yes." For advocates pushing from outside on either "higher ups" or directly responsible officials, it never hurts to remind them of the idealistic or public service reasons that were at least part of why they initially ran for office. It also helps to know your facts – the scope and costs of the problem to both the most-impacted groups and society at large, the technical and financial feasibility of the desired reforms, the likelihood it will have the intended impact, the types of opposition you face, the value to the decision-maker and his agency of going along with your demands, and the political risks of only partial success or even failure.

Sometimes, all it takes is the "insider politics" of a conversation or phone call. If you or someone connected with your issue already has a relationship with the appropriate decision-makers, you can simply present your case – although figuring out who is the right person to "make the ask" and how to convince her to "call in that chit" can be a complicated process. This tactic is more likely to work if advocates have inside allies among an agency's senior staff who can echo your arguments during staff meetings.

At other times you have to first catch decision-makers' attention, which typically requires raising your voice in some way and mobilizing allies to exert pressure.

SUPPLEMENTARY STRATEGIES

There are other ways to generate, or at least to strengthen, political will. Sometimes the key is reducing fear of the unknown. Getting the agency to set up low-cost pilot projects that demonstrate the feasibility and non-threatening nature of proposed changes can reduce opposition from decision-makers or other opponents. Janette Sadik-Khan, former New York City Commissioner of Transportation, installed "pilot" and "temporary" plazas and bike lanes all across the city, where most of them quickly became an accepted part of the landscape.

This doesn't negate all opposition – particularly from those whose rigid ideological beliefs require them to ignore proven facts. But, for many people, seeing is believing. Creating "facts-on-the-ground" can be used to undercut required processes – for better and worse. But it can also provide the basis for evidence-based discussion. When Massachusetts became one of the first states to legalize same-sex marriage and the "predicted" collapse of heterosexual families didn't occur, it became harder for cultural reactionaries in other states to use similar tactics. (This of course, doesn't eliminate the fall back "*there* is different from *here*" argument.)

However, instead of directly and visibly pushing for your own issue, it's sometimes possible to hitch a ride in a rear car of someone else's train, hoping that their momentum and victory will create a chance to slip through your own goals as part of the package. The ban on gender discrimination in college sports was piggybacked into the 1964 Civil Rights Act, added as a mocking absurdity by an opposing Southern representative but then quickly absorbed into the evolving bill by its sponsors. Repeal of the Clinton-era ban on the construction of new public housing was slipped into a military funding bill by Representative Alexandria Ocasio-Cortez. In the electoral arena, voters are primarily swayed by a candidate's top three or four positions, with very little attention paid to the ideas in the small print at the bottom. Some politicians come into office trailing an invisible list of otherwise unpassable policies – few of Donald Trump's supporters had any idea how much he'd use his office for personal profit. Still, there is no reason that progressives can't also use this same process for good effect.

CRISIS IS OPPORTUNITY
Advocates should always be ready to take advantage of a crisis. Emergencies are, by definition, a moment when past practices are obviously not working. The bigger the emergency the broader the scope of policies and programs people are willing to see changed. A sudden catastrophe loosens traditional roadblocks and makes everyone more receptive to new ideas. The disaster of Hurricane Sandy made the entire Northeast more willing to discuss coastal management issues. A region-wide

blackout makes it a lot easier to push for energy-resilience strategies. Both President G.W. Bush and NYC Mayor Rudy Giuliani were in political tailspins until the 9/11 attacks thrust them into the spotlight and induced a traumatized population to rally behind them – which opened the door for a flood of conservative initiatives having nothing to do with national security.

But crisis opportunities must be seized. Advocates need to have at least a few "shovel ready" plans. The incremental progress that advocacy achieves are also pre-crisis preparation. In most cases the groundwork for abrupt progress must be laid beforehand – ideas must be tested, legitimized through endorsements from at least a few mainstream experts, and then publicized. In fact, even short of a full-blown crisis, long years of patient effort followed by sudden success triggered by an unanticipated event turns out to be a pretty common advocacy pattern. (And not just in advocacy: the founder of a successful 1980s high-tech dotcom I once worked at commented that business success "is a long series of failures followed by a lucky accident.")

In short, mobilizing political will among decision-making officials almost always requires a long, persistent, and multi-faceted advocacy campaign. And if all else fails, you can always run for office yourself.

Ensuring Agency Capacity

The newer or more innovative the change that has been won, the more disruptive it is of past practices, the less likely it is that an agency's current staff know how to implement it – much less do it really well. For both social welfare programs and physical construction, what is needed are skills and experience handling the entire life cycle – design, creation or construction, operation, long-term maintenance, and evaluation. The multi-year complexity of this process is another reason why advocates sometimes discover that getting something initially approved is the easy part.

Some agency insiders may have been secretly cheering on (or even helping) the advocacy effort and welcome the chance to do what they've been hoping for – some may even have developed some expertise. On the other hand, it is quite possible that other members of the agency's staff have spent years opposing the very thing they are now being told to implement. It may be necessary to pull in people from other departments, hire different consultants, or reach outside through (well-structured) public-private-nonprofit partnerships. When Boston first began making bike lanes part of its road markings, there wasn't a single city or vendor transportation engineer around who had ever actually designed a real bike lane. Advocates reached out to a couple of small firms with relevant experience in other parts of the country, urging them to set up a Boston office and then demanding that established vendors subcontract them.

Of course, if the new policy, program, or infrastructure works out well, the staff skeptics will probably come around – and be deserving of credit for doing so.

MOVING IN

Advocates know that the worst thing that can happen to a new idea is for its first example to be done poorly – which means that the implementing staff needs to go beyond formal acquiescence to genuine enthusiasm. (It doesn't hurt to have political leaders make it clear that this is a "not allowed to fail" project.) This is one reason that successful advocacy occasionally results in the advocates seeking to get hired to create or run what they've won, either taking over key parts of the agency or creating a new one. NYC Transportation Commissioner Sadik-Khan hired a large number of transportation advocates who had the vision and distance from past official practice that she needed. New York quickly became the national leader in surface transportation safety and mobility improvements for every mode, including walking, bicycling, bus, and the reclamation of street space for urban living.

Of course, once you're in charge of something, the longer you stay the harder it is to denounce its failures. It's now your job to deal with the compromises caused by budget limits, political constraints, demands for visible short-term results, and the need to balance the interests of a variety of stakeholders. Even worse, employees do not control the goals or values of their organization. In the public sector, voters, expressing their desires through the election of legislative and executive candidates, are the theoretical source of general direction. In the business world, the CEO rules. In both spheres, beyond the underlying commitment to constitutional rights and legal precedents, everyone's first political loyalty is supposed to be to the official under whom they serve.

Still, if power is the key to change, it is difficult – perhaps unethical – to refuse to seize that which you can. Moving from "outside the system" to an inside position allows you to make a real difference in some people's lives. It is often possible for assertive leaders and staffers to push the boundaries of past practices and advocate for improvements. Still, when doing so, it is hard to avoid the trap of "advocacy capture," in which once-radical drivers of change become entombed within the still-inadequate status quo. (This is the opposite of "agency capture," in which a regulatory agency ends up promoting and protecting the profits and power of the businesses it was supposed to oversee.)

OUTSIDE INSIDERS
Of course, you don't have to be an employee to work for or with an agency or program. Consultants, advisors, and members of "special commissions" are all able to impact the way that policies are written and programs are designed and implemented. However, even these more arms-length roles contain constraints.

As a paid consultant your first loyalty – and a precondition of ever getting hired again -- is to whomever hired you. So long as you are not being asked to break any laws or professional standards, it is your responsibility to be a trustworthy and dependable team member. But it is often difficult to separate the threads: are you working for the person or the agency, for the politically at-tuned top officials or for the more long-term program staff? And what do they really want from you – justification for what they already want to do or new ideas, real evaluation of past efforts and future impacts or excuses for the status quo? From an advo-cacy perspective, the questions for progressive consultants are how far you can push beyond the limits of what those you work for want to hear -- how to leverage your status as the "outside expert." The tension between purity and pragmatism can be complicated.

Official advisory committees, established by statute or regula-tion and attached to an office, program, or agency are, in many cases, legally an extension of the agency being advised, which imposes a variety of "open meeting" and conflict of interest con-trols on what you are allowed to say or do. Often, your most useful function is to support progressive staff, helping push their plans through a resistant bureaucracy. However, even if the staff you are advising is part of the problem, members of an official advisory committee are usually not supposed to publicly disagree with the people or agency they are "working for" – an ethical (and sometimes legal) limit that has led to my resigna-tion from at least one advisory committee in my home town.

Ad-hoc advisory committees are "unofficial" bodies informally created to provide feedback and brainstorming to help agency staff. It is also assumed that their presence helps legitimize the policy or program under discussion among key constituen-cies. Sometimes, their purpose is to review and then speak for the adoption of staff proposals by higher levels of the agency or other decision-making bodies. Committee members are rela-tively free to voice their personal opinions, but the assumption is that if they have major objections they will simply resign.

Of course, consultants and advisors of all types have one more advocacy option – to go public with their opinions and accept the consequences. A "minority report" or dissenting public statement can capture headlines (unauthorized "leaks" can also be effective), although these usually tend to be followed by a resignation, or even a prosecution. In some cases, this can derail a really bad idea. Daniel Ellsberg helped stop a war. However, often, the newsworthy relevance of a departing expert is short-lived, the consequences of insubordination long-lasting.

BLUE RIBBONS

Probably the greatest freedom and leverage is held by members of a high-level "blue-ribbon panel" or "special commission" assembled around a specific, relatively short-term task in situations where top decision-makers feel there is no consensus about the nature of a problem or its solution, or where they need political cover for implementing their preferred solution in a contentious political environment. To serve their political function, people asked to be members of that type of commission are usually professionally prestigious, technically expert, or well known – and therefore have a base of legitimacy (and income) outside their appointment. Their status, and often the serious nature of the issue they've been asked to address, gives them space to raise difficult questions and reach conclusions somewhat independently of the desires of the appointing authority. Perhaps the most famous example of this was Nobel laureate Richard Feynman's public embarrassment of both military and NASA big shots on the Commission appointed to investigate the Space Shuttle Challenger's horrific explosion. His live, televised demonstration of the problem caused by freezing O-rings destroyed their self-protective denials.

Even special commission staff are relatively free. I served as staff to a Panel convened by Governor Mike Dukakis after his humiliating defeat in the 1988 presidential election. The state economy, like the nation's, was slipping out of the previous years' boom and he wanted new, politically viable ideas about using the public sector as a stimulus. I was able to access nearly any department, collect any data, and ask any question I wanted. (As it turned out, the Panel's chairperson, a banker, was primarily interested in finding ways to reduce spending and consolidate agencies, ignoring Dukakis' desires. And the reform and revitalization ideas I collected never left my notebook.)

WORKING FROM WITHIN

Even during quiet periods of "business as usual," internal advocates lay the basis for future partnerships – and improve their organization's effectiveness at the same time. One tactic is to open the edges of organizations to new voices – including the people most affected by agency policies and knowledgeable outside advocates. For example, the Massachusetts Department of Transportation has an open attendance policy and "speaking rights" at its Road Design Exception Review Committee – which approves (or rejects) requests to violate the state's Complete Streets policy design guidelines. In addition, the proposed Exception Requests are posted online and people unable to attend the meetings are also able to send in comments – which are taken into account by the voting staff members. The result is a much more thorough and creative discussion of options.

Day-to-day interaction with advocates is also an opportunity for staff to help the advocates understand the constraints affecting agency staff. At the same time, friendly advocates are in a good position to call for things that agency staff can't publicly talk about, such as budget or staff increases as well as new types of authorization.

Inside allies can help legitimize advocates' efforts by acknowledging their contributions and catalytic role. And smart advocates know to return the favor by making sure their allies have a chance to correct problems before they have to face public criticism or protest actions – and then publicly thanking key agency staff and praising agency programs and projects for doing the right thing.

UNLEASHING PUBLIC CREATIVITY

Agency capacity is – or should be – about more than technical expertise and experience. Part of the mission of every public agency in a democratic society should be strengthening the democracy that it serves. This requires, among other things, institutions whose operations are designed to foster effective cooperation, honest communication, mutual respect, and inclusive community both among agency staff and between the staff and the public, particularly those populations most affected by the issues the institution addresses. Shaping organizational culture, mission, and operations to embrace this broader vision requires both outside pressure and internal leadership in four ways:

First, the organization needs to welcome new ideas from both within and without. Internally, there should be ways for employee ideas to get an audience with top-level decision-makers without having to climb through the constrictions of their supervisory chain of command. Externally, there should be ways for nonprofessional "outsiders" – advocates, citizens living with a problem or in a situation, or the general public – to present new ideas to senior leaders, no matter how unorthodox: periodic "listening sessions" for example.

Second, public organizations need to provide support for citizen-initiated pilot projects – helping flesh out ideas into proposals and then into projects. Some foundations have created "innovation charrettes" where local groups can get technical assistance – and perhaps even a small budget – for fleshing out and testing an idea. But why not make this a city activity focused on self-help or neighborhood improvement ideas? Just as enterprise forums allow would-be entrepreneurs to pitch their ideas to potential investors, cities can set up "citizen initiative forums" where people can pitch ideas to city agencies that have budget and authorization to try them. Cambridge's "participatory budgeting" process uses a joint citizen-agency committee to sift through public suggestions and then runs an open-to-all-residents vote to decide which get selected for city implementation. This requires public acceptance that along with all the good ideas will come some really bad ones; and that those failures can be dealt with and learned from.

Third, cities need to monitor these experiments and adopt the best for city-wide implementation. Just as states (and cities) can be laboratories of democracy for the national government, citizen initiatives can be seen as a testing ground of ideas for city (and state) government use. One strategy is simply to repeat a successful pilot in other places. Another is to provide a general implementation blueprint for use by other neighborhoods and organizations, along with technical assistance and (perhaps) financial support – but allow the adopters to adapt the idea in any way that better serves their own needs. This approach can even work with large city-scale and regional projects. Urban planning visionary Jan Gehl suggests creating "Frameworks" – clear and authoritative plans for needed large-scale infrastructure structure providing for incremental creation that intentionally leaves many details unanswered, allowing space and time for each group of implementers to make their own choices as the project evolves over the coming years.

Finally, all this is more likely to work if cities build experimentation into their regular programs, reserving some percentage of every budget for tests, trials, pilots, and other temporary projects – the best of which create some kind of physical, political, or cultural space for the public to use for its own purposes. New ideas provoke a greater fear of the unknown than a small-scale physical reality, so these temporary installations are a good way to work through the NIMBY horrors – although it still doesn't solve the "great idea, but not here" problem.

Securing Institutional Permanence

What happens when the next mayor, governor, or president is elected, when the next CEO or division director gets hired, or the next headline pushes a new issue into the limelight? In most institutions or programs, innovation is seldom initially executed across the entire system. Instead, new ideas are usually set up as "pilots" on the fringes of an organization's normal hierarchies and budgets. Even in the private sector, creating an offsite "skunk works" is a traditional route to creativity, with the development of the IBM PC a prime example. Occasionally, these on-the-side experiments are phenomenally successful and get heroically repatriated into the parent organization. More typically, the project flourishes for a while under an interested elected official, agency head, or corporate executive's protection and then, when that patron leaves it is either spun off or, more typically, allowed to quietly run out of steam and fade away.

Therefore, from the beginning, every advocacy campaign needs to think about how to transform its desired change from a pilot into a practice, from an experiment into a norm, from a one-off to an assumed component of business as usual. Ironically, as much as bureaucracy is the opposite of direct democracy, once your proposals have been adopted, bureaucracy can help protect them from the likely pushback. Advocates have to ensure that the lessons and methods of their project are deliberately folded back into the organization's staffing patterns, work plans, budget requests, performance evaluations, and public image. Or else their success will disappear the moment they do.

Institutionalization is largely an inside operation, although it is much more likely to actually happen if there is continuing outside pressure. Still, there is no substitute for internal champions in a position to push for revising training programs, budget defaults, job descriptions, and evaluation criteria -- which is another reason for going to work for an agency! In government, outgoing administrations try to box in their successors by rushing to make appointments and sign contracts. In business, program leaders try to get their milestones included in corporate strategic plans and staff performance reviews. In the non-profit world, projects can be spun off into their own organizations or transferred to public agencies.

VICTORY OUT OF DEFEAT, DEFEAT OUT OF VICTORY

Unfortunately, permanence isn't actually permanent. Major victories or defeats of one era lay the basis for future defeats or victories in the next. Conditions change. New alliances emerge. No victory is final. No defeat permanent. The bottom line is that even after apparent victory, advocacy must continue. And somehow, in the midst of it all, advocates must find time and energy to celebrate. As Emma Goldman said (and as it's important to repeat), "if you can't dance, it's not my revolution."

SECTION IV:
WORKING WITHIN LARGER CURRENTS

Often, our behavior is shaped by subtle pressures around us, but we fail to recognize those pressures. Thus, we mistakenly believe that our behavior emanates from some inner disposition...
DR. TIMOTHY WILSON "WE ARE WHAT WE DO," *THIS EXPLAINS EVERYTHING*

And it was about being true to the fact, that many things in life -- oh so many more than we think -- can never be explained at all.
GRAHAM SWIFT, MOTHERING SUNDAY

9. THEORIES OF CHANGE:
Why Things Happen

10. MAKING SENSE OF CONTEXT:
Weaving Your Way Through
Local Reality

11. CULTURE AND STABILITY:
Majoritarian Inertia and
Social Tectonics

9. THEORIES OF CHANGE:
Why Things Happen

*Men make their own history, but they do not make it as they please;
they do not make it under self-selected circumstances, but under circumstances existing already, given and transmitted from the past.*
KARL MARX, THE EIGHTEENTH BRUMAIRE OF LOUIS BONA-
PARTE

Standing in one spot, the breezes blow randomly from every direction, deflected by everything in the local context: trees, hills,
buildings, heat islands, and more. But we know that there are
larger-scale patterns beyond our immediate perception. Understanding them makes it possible to harness their power. The
discovery of the Trade Winds transformed long-distance navi-
gation. Mapping the Jet Stream transformed weather prediction
and air travel.

While our individual lives often feel buffeted by seemingly random impacts from every direction, these deeper currents also
flow within human history. The persistent questions are about
their nature, their relationship to each other, and each of their
levels of determinism. To what amount does one or more of
these hidden dynamics control the way history and our individual lives play out, and therefore what it is likely (if not inevitable) that the future will bring? It is probable that, ultimately,
the universe's existence is just a series of random accidents. It
is probable that there is no moral arc of history to climb. But in
the swirling of events there are patterns. And as meaning-seek-
ing humans, we look for those patterns to help us plan for what
is to come, to help prepare ourselves for effective action. This
is less about history itself -- a description of past decisions and
action as understood and experienced by those who lived it -- as
it is using the past as the raw material of origin stories we create
to give depth to our understanding and aspirations of present
experience. But it is not only mythologizing; the past does blow
into the future. And it is much easier to move with the wind at

your back.

At one of my college reunions, a former history-major classmate told me that he now understood why we studied the past: it was to be prepared to see how God's will played out in human affairs. In a strangely parallel manner, dogmatic Marxists hold that the future of human society is predetermined by the inescapable rules of capitalist economic development, inevitably leading from increased concentrations of wealth amidst general immiseration to revolutionary well-being.

For those of us less blinded by religious fundamentalism or political metaphysics, the question of causation is less easily answered and future events less easily predicted. We know from biology as much as from history that even though some things remain the same, change is the only constant; from physics as much as from philosophy that reality is ultimately unknowable; from logic as much as from experience that the future is both constrained by the past and open-ended. We have to accept the cognitive dissonance of knowing that there are broad patterns and forces while at the same time accepting that it's all riddled with happenstance, that trends can be anticipated but nothing is inevitable. Like far-sea sailors, we need to both pay attention to the weather and never forget it's our choices about rudder setting and sail placement that will set our course.

There are many theories about what drives history. Progressive politics is rooted in the belief that society is primarily shaped by people power – the cumulative collective activity of ordinary folks. In contrast, most traditional history, and much of the media coverage of today's political scene, is written from the perspective of leaders – their personalities, the choices they make, and their ability to project their power onto society. From a political economy perspective, society is shaped by the internal, advantage-seeking, financial underpinnings of production, distribution, and consumption systems. Or maybe it's nature that creates opportunities and limits – the presence of water or a sudden natural disaster.

Winds From Every Quarter

Causality is a complex concept. Still, theories of overall historical change tend to fall into four groups: top-down, bottom-up, outside-in, and inside-out. Each describes at least some aspects of social dynamics. In that sense they are all "true." While one pattern, one type of influence, may predominate at one time or in one place, they are all ever-present and impactful, directly or indirectly, immediately or over the long term, dramatically or invisibly. French Marxist, Louis Althusser, took the idea of "overdetermination" from Freud, revising it to mean that significant structural change seldom occurs until there are so many pressures that society has run out of ways to avoid dealing with the underlying issue. This makes more flexible social systems more resilient. It also creates a strategic opportunity to speed up the process. Campaigns for change are more likely to be successful if they are prepared to take advantage of, and avoid the traps created by, each type of the four change dynamics.

In addition, the degree to which each dynamic is relevant to a particular campaign will vary according to the level of the power hierarchy being targeted, the issues that are being addressed, and the balance of personal transformation versus societal change the campaign's organizing style encourages. By analyzing the context in terms of each of the change dynamics at various times during a campaign, advocates will be better able to pinpoint the current location of power over the needed decisions, possible tensions among the decision-making networks, sources of potential leverage -- and therefore the best strategies to use, potential allies to reach out to, and the most useful actions to take.

Top-down theories start with Great Men but also include a range of insider politics: power elites, conspiracies, connections, and corruption. Good leaders create good societies. But, good or bad, rulers rule. Top-down power dynamics are the environment within which most advocacy takes place. It is an important reality to understand and deal with.

Bottom-up theories see the actions of "the people" (defined in various ways) and their organizations as the force that ultimately moves society forward. It includes perspectives ranging from the view that all history is just "people being people" to the view that all democratic change comes from political mass movements. Social change strategies based on this perspective include pragmatic local organizing around immediate needs; leading by catalytic example; public education to change culture and consciousness; creating progressive political parties; as well as "mass strikes" and other forms of mass mobilizations. Most of this book concerns ways to strengthen advocates' agency in the context of bottom-up strategies.

Inside-out analyses focus on the internal dynamics of human-created systems – with change either moving outwards from the inherent tensions at the core of a system, or inwards from the fringe as various populations react to the system's failure. New technologies can sometimes exacerbate these dynamics in radically destabilizing ways. In stable times, standard interest group politics produce enough reforms to keep things going. During crises, governing elites unable to deal with that level of disruption break apart into self-serving factions, opening the way for more inclusive alliances and new institutions. (Chapter 10, on the need to understand and work with surrounding societal trends, more deeply explores the organizing implications of inside-out dynamics.)

Outside-in proponents, like Jared Diamond in *Guns, Germs, and Steel*, point out that external limits -- geography, location, natural resources, and climate – are the ultimate shapers of what societies have been able to do and become. And natural disasters – from earthquakes to falling asteroids – can create unmanageable shocks to the system. Open plains allow migration and invasions; mountains and oceans create walls. Differing geographic distribution of resources promotes commerce; differing germs spread conquest-facilitating pandemics. Good soil, timely rains, and mild climates prompt agriculture and population growth; droughts and storms and soil depletion create famine and collapse.

The joke attributed to Mark Twain – "Everybody talks about the weather, but nobody does anything about it" – is funny exactly because we all know that there isn't anything that anyone can do about it except to protect yourself. But, ironically, that is no longer true in the Anthropocene era. Nature's limits will be increasingly relevant and visible as climate change reshapes our physical and social landscapes.

Inside-Out

Inside-out theories are the most complex. In general, they see macro-level systems – the economy, technology, governance, international relations, culture, and others -- as having internal tensions, contradictions, divergent tendencies, and life-cycle crisis points. The boom-then-bust cycle of capitalism both rejuvenates the economy and creates widespread suffering with accompanying instability. Democracy both promises equality and provides a cover for rulers to create hierarchal systems of "representation" that allow them to generally do what they want. Nations need each other for trade and coordination of common resources like the atmosphere, but compete with each other for dominance and preferential access to resources. All these inside-the-system dynamics cause conflicts and disruptions that ripple outwards across entire societies and even the world. The details of each situation vary according to the particularities of place and time. Proponents of inside-out theories of social change include adherents of a wide variety of systems as the primary driver and end up in a variety of political camps: both right-wing free-market and Marxist dogmatists, both cultural chauvinists and techno-utopians, determinists and hyper-voluntarists.

Like the weather, the fact that we live inside macro-systems makes us often experience them as "givens" – impersonal, permanent, external forces that we simply have to live within. The economy. Technology. The governance system. The educational system. It is what it is.

This is, in fact, exactly the perspective that elites try to inculcate in their subjects – the status quo is unchangeable; there is no alternative; now is forever. And there is some truth to this, particularly in pre-industrial societies. Speaking of the many centuries of the Roman Empire, in her book *SPQR*, Mary Beard writes that systems in that long-lasting society were much more influential than the people who ran them.

> *Not to say that everything remained the same...[but] there was a remarkably stable structure of rule and a remarkably stable set of problems and tensions across the whole period... there is no sign at all that the character of the ruler affected the basic template of government...in any significant way...*

In contrast, as analyzed by economist Joseph Schumpeter, modern industrial capitalism grows partly by eating itself, a process of "creative destruction" and constant re-invention. Schumpeter saw this as a strength: particular corporations or technologies may come and go, but markets and profit-seeking innovation grow better. However, it is enormously disruptive to those trampled in the process – and projecting a perception of permanence and stability in the overall society is a constant concern of rulers. In the twentieth century, this was wrapped up in the Anglo-American world through what Indian essayist Pankaj Mishra calls "liberal triumphalism" – the presumption, starting during the later stages of the British Empire and carried over into the "American Century" after WWI "that Western-style liberal democracy will be absorbed by the rest of the world...[seeing] the highly contingent achievements of our culture as the final form and norm of human existence." (*Bland Fanatics: Liberals, Race, and Empire*)

While understanding and publicizing these systemic processes, it is also vital that advocacy organizers help people – themselves and others – remember that we are not "locked in." Every one of these systems is made by human actions and decisions – and therefore capable of being changed.

LEVERAGING TENSION

Internal systemic dynamics can both spur growth but also potentially rip the system apart. This presents advocate organizers with several challenges. First is to grasp the power of the surrounding systems over people's behavior and beliefs without getting dragged into a deterministic belief in the inevitability of its continuation – no matter how established or entrenched, history does not ever end. Techno innovation solves some problems but creates others.

Second is to understand the system's internal dynamics well enough to see the opportunities created by shifts in its internal power relationships to create new alliances and additional victories. Capitalism continually cycles from boom to bust and back again and again, each one shaking up the relative power of various elite factions. Third is to be prepared for those moments when the system's internal contradictions or its mismatch with the surrounding environment lead to crises – the door-opening moments when radical change is possible.

POLITICAL DYNAMICS

No matter their nature, political systems are, in general, designed to maintain the status quo while allowing occasional tweaks to keep things humming. At the same time, they often contain their own internal tensions, inefficiencies, and competitive dynamics that allow occasional upsurges of mass discontent to force adjustments (changes) in policy, and improvements in the general population's well-being.

The United States' federal, multi-branch, and hierarchal system of governance was deliberately designed to make federal and even state government policies slow to change. A representational hierarchy helps coordinate a varied, dispersed, and very contentious population. It also creates endless opportunities for elites at every level to dominate their immediate political process through the use of their wealth to shape election outcomes and government decisions.

At the same time, our nation's size, wealth, and diversity – as well as our enormously multi-layered confusion of governments -- have created a uniquely varied and large nation-wide network of overlapping but distinct local, regional, and national elites. The disconnection of all those pieces of government, as well as the occasional friction between those elite groups, has created room for people to push states and municipalities to move beyond what was possible on the national level, for states to be "the laboratories of democracy." Efforts to create unemployment insurance, public health, workplace safety were all initiated at state and city levels where working families were most able to exert pressure.

In fact, it is exactly the playing out of this internal contradiction that has helped make the United States so amazingly resilient despite repeated crises. Its resources and redundancies provide sufficient flexibility to adapt to changing contexts, work around internal conflicts, and allow factions of the elite to build more inclusive alliances, even if the side effects have been brutal to particular subordinate groups – African-Americans, immigrants, Native Americans, women, workers, and poor people in general.

One manifestation of this internal tension is between two competing sets of interpretation of citizenship, peoplehood, and the nation. From the beginning, the United States has been what Frederick Douglas called a "composite nation" composed of indigenous people who were already here, people who came by choice (even if desperate), and those brought in chains. And it quickly developed hierarchies of rich and poor, urban and rural, male and female, and more. Its diversity made it, in historian and journalist Jill Lepore's analysis, more a political and civic alliance of different groups who embrace a common (even if invented) mythology as part of the glue holding them together than a "people who share a common descent," more of a state working to become a nation than a nation-state. (*This Is America*)

ACCIDENTAL UNIVERSALISM

From the beginning, there has been constant conflict over where to draw the nation's definitional demographic lines.   The Founding Fathers – rich white males – understood that even their own ranks were composed of people from a variety of backgrounds. They liked to think of the new country they were starting as a sanctuary of liberty, business opportunity unhindered by royal privileges, and safety -- a welcoming home for those like them regardless of what part of endlessly warring Europe they were coming from. Very few of them were either democrats or equalitarians.

However, it was exactly because the Founding Fathers saw themselves as leaders of the entire society, as representing everyone, as embodying in themselves all of "we the people," that the documents and the political system they created were written in such universal terms. "All men are created equal" – an historically precedent-breaking basis for citizenship! Ironically and fortunately, it was that arrogant assumption that gave the ideals and values they expressed in those foundational documents such unlimited democratic implications.

The universal terminology of American ideals and political rights, no matter how constricted in practice, has been a motivating force for successive waves of popular protest within this country. They have legitimized demands for inclusion into the mainstream of society by one marginalized group after another, from immigrants to former slaves, from women to homosexuals. The Declaration of Independence and the American Revolution's embedding of sovereignty in the people rather than in the divine rights of the aristocracy or of the faithful of a particular creed, has provided an inspiring vision for democratic movements around the globe for hundreds of years.

It is in this tension between universal ideals and repressive reality that progressive organizing has room to build. But utilizing the gap requires framing demands in exactly the universal terms that America culture makes sacred. Martin Luther King Jr. said, "I have a dream that one day this nation will rise up and live out the true meaning of its creed." It can't be simple rhetoric: what is being advocated has to be something that is good for everyone, even if it is "more good" for a particular subgroup. In fact, nearly every demand by a new group for inclusion and a chance to move up the well-being ladder will be unsettling to those groups a short distance above it – the groups whose own precarious well-being has depended on finding some accommodation with the existing status quo. The only way to convince them that additional change is desirable is to stress that they, too, will be the beneficiaries.

Marginalized groups fighting for both a positive self-identity and systemic responsiveness walk a delicate path. They have specific histories and needs that they need addressed by both themselves and the surrounding society. At the same time, sectoral or group-specific demands are extremely unlikely to be supported by anyone else. Historian Michael Kazin notes that it's hard to find "any American radical or reformer who repudiated the national belief system and still had a major impact on U.S. politics and policy." Advocates who ignore the heritage of expanding human rights that is one strand of American history, who narrowly focus on their own particularistic issues or benefits, reduce their chance of success.

Top-Down

Every society has ancient stories of the world-shaping exploits of gods, kings, and heroes. It's possible that seeing power as an attribute of people above us is based on our infant experience of parental dependence. Our current obsession with celebrities regardless of the basis for their prominence is a modern version of projecting our awe on people who seem to have powers we lack. Similarly, the classic version of history hinges on the role of Great Men (with a smattering of women) whose genius, courage, ability, and charisma shape our collective reality.

Obviously, although there were always other forces also in play – overdetermination at work -- certain people have played a crucial role in history: from Genghis Khan to Stalin, from the Emperor Meiji to Franklin Roosevelt, from Julius Caesar to Winston Churchill, and many more. It is hard to imagine that European history wouldn't be significantly different without Napoleon or Hitler; hard to imagine the US without Lincoln, or China without Mao. It would have been easy for George Washington to accept a kingship, to have allowed the creation of a republican aristocracy, or to just stay in office for the rest of his life – and US history would have flowed down a different path.

The celebration of toughness at the top is not confined to politics. We already lionize the entrepreneur who breaks the rules, disrupts markets, and attacks anything that stands in his way. Uber's founder was a self-described "pirate" loyal to nothing besides his own ship; the billions that corporation is now worth is considered proof of the correctness of his approach, despite the founder's resignation after run-ins with the #me-too movement.

There is a profound need for good leadership in every organization and society. But the emergence in society of a widespread yearning for a "big man" to take charge is often a response to a population-wide feeling of desperation, a sense that our lives are becoming dangerously (or simply humiliatingly) out of our control. The more unsettled the general conditions, the greater the feeling of insecurity and fear, the more people begin looking for a hero, a strong man; someone who can play the political role of cognitive linguist George Lakoff's "strict father" who will take charge, protect the public family, be tough and powerful, push through problems, and make things safely "right" again (perhaps even "great again"). This is the public demand to which authoritarians respond. And because we are human, it can happen anywhere. Donald Trump's political cousins are taking office in countries around the globe; his acolytes are digging in around the US.

OPPORTUNITY MAKES THE MAN

Sometimes it feels like the situation seems to create the person who "rises" to the occasion – i.e., if that particular person wasn't there, someone else would have emerged to fill the void. But often a situation doesn't feel so overly determined. Francis Sargent was an accidental governor of Massachusetts, moving up in 1969 from being Lieutenant Governor when Governor John Volpe became Richard Nixon's Secretary of Transportation. Despite angry opposition from his predecessor, Sargent embraced the demands of the growing anti-highway protests and became the first governor in the nation to stop construction of urban interstate highway extensions. It is very possible that the urban destruction caused by highway construction would have eventually led to a halt in any case, if only because of the escalating protests and opponents' "People's Lobby" visits to elected officials. But there was nothing inevitable about that decision at that time. Sargent made a choice that another person might not have made, and things changed.

Often, a person's unique importance isn't obvious until he or she is no longer there. In Chicago, Harold Washington was able to unite a broad coalition of reformers and became the city's first African-American mayor, displacing the deeply entrenched old-ethnic patronage machine. His unexpected heart attack at the beginning of his second term revealed his pivotal role in smoothing over the lack of deeper unity among his supporters and led to their rapid electoral decline – including the rebuilding of the old Daley family political machine. There really are people who direct events down one specific path, who shape the future in ways that wouldn't have happened were they not in charge.

And having a friend in high places can be decisive. One of the lessons of historian Erik Loomis' book, *A History of America in Ten Strikes*, is that the active opposition of government makes working class struggles almost impossible to win; some level of support, or even just neutrality, is usually a precondition for victory. We are now living in a political era in which disagreements are treated as a no-holds-barred "war" saturated with violence, racism, misogyny, and cynical nationalism. Government's role in coming conflicts will be vital. A good leader, with a solid base and a progressive outlook, is worth supporting even if he or she isn't perfect.

THE REBEL PRINCE

Top-down change sometimes comes where there is dissent among factions of the current elites escalates to the point that one or more of the dissident leaders reaches out to the broader population for support. The "rebels" offer both a critique of the more dominant groups (which creates political space for even more radical analyses of what's wrong) and resources (media access, funds, connections to friends within government) that help mobilize existing and potential insurgencies from below. The dynamic is most relevant in tightly controlled authoritarian societies. Russian journalist Vadim Nikitin points out that in his country, "civil society actions can succeed only when they're able to ally with one elite group against another" ("The New Civic Activism in Russia," *The Nation*, 11/8/2010).

In fact, the "rebel prince" is a common theme in many uprisings starting with Moses, Pharaoh's adopted son. FDR came from a family of American aristocrats. The British Suffragists were notable for their upper-class leadership. During the Indochina wars of the 1950s and 60s, all three factions of the Laotian civil wars – the Royalists, Neutralists, and Communists – were led by princes of the ruling family.

POWER ELITES

Individual Great Men may actually be part of an enabling network. Radical sociologist C. Wright Mills wrote that while "people at the top" make polite nods and some accommodation to public perceptions and democratic participation, decisions are really made by a "power elite" whose influence comes from their leadership of society's major institutions. While occasionally open to properly acculturated new recruits, the power elite is primarily drawn from families with either inherited or not-too-newly-acquired wealth or status; and the primary function of the institutions they run is to maintain a world supportive of those privileges. While the decision-makers have enormous power within their own institutions, they have to operate in a competitive environment full of other actors always eager to gain at their expense. Inter-elite struggles and aggressive negotiations are as much part of their world as social cohesion. And sometimes their particular basis of power fails.

As today's world economy is jarringly transformed by the global reach, data processing, analytic power, and algorithmic decision-making capabilities of digital technology, old industries are being blown apart and new ones are appearing in an incredibly short period of time. In little more than a decade, nine digital companies, most of them relatively new, have come to dominate both commercial (US) and political control (China) domains. In the USA it's FANGAMI (Facebook, Amazon, Netflix, Google/Alphabet, Apple, Microsoft, IBM). In China it's BATX (Baidu, Alibaba, Tencent, and Xioami). Collectively, they are already rich enough to eliminate competition by buying most new research or threatening technologies as well as any start-up poised to compete. In nearly every sector of the American economy, three or fewer firms control 80% to 90% of the business. In another generation the new family fortunes will integrate their children into the elite private schools, summer camps, colleges, fraternities, and social groups that nurture upper class relationships.

Strategies for progressive change based on this view of power relationships place a major emphasis on taking advantage of conflicts between different sectors of the elite in order to gain allies, and framing demands so that they serve the interests of those allies as well as your own. The push for school lunches, the main source of nutrition for millions of low-income children, was framed in ways that accented the benefits for farmers, which allowed farm-state Congressmen to support it – despite the non-nutritious compromises this forced advocates to accept, it was (correctly) seen as a stepping stone for future upgrades.

CONSPIRATORIAL DETOURS

Unfortunately, it is easier to see elite dynamics as top-down conspiracies rather than as part of systemic processes. It is much easier to imagine a small cabal secretly plotting together than to visualize a decentralized process in which a huge number of autonomous actors with varying degrees of power and often conflicting immediate interests independently make decisions that in the aggregate create an invisible web of society-wide socio-economic power relationships that encompasses and shapes everyone's life, including your own. Conspiracy theorists see government primarily as a cover for the secret manipulations of small groups of evil manipulators. History is merely the playing out of the conspirators' self-interested machinations. Exposing the existence and operations of the hidden plots is their path towards change.

Having entered the realm of imagined reality, conspiracists can find endless confirmations of the presence of the chosen manipulators -- the Illuminati, the Free Masons, the Roman Catholic Church, the Communists, the Trilateral Commission, the United Nations, and the Jews, to name just a few currently being denounced in far-right circles. The belief that "everything is fixed against me/us" feeds their prejudices: from racism to anti-Semitism, from nativist nationalism to white supremacy. Adherents' feelings of exclusion, paranoia, and belief in an invisible but totally surrounding destructiveness lead them towards extreme actions, including vigilante violence.

Motivating conspiracy paranoia is often, according to journalist David Aaronowitch in *Voodoo Histories*,

> *an externalization of internal fears about alternations to the passing world...Conspiracy theory may be one way of reclaiming power and disclaiming responsibility... [Expressing] both admiration and envy, much of the later unconscious.... formulated by the politically defeated and taken up by the socially defeated.*

It is hard, and probably a waste of time, to try to argue conspiracists out of their theories, since they are usually based on a set of beliefs and emotional attitudes rather than on facts, and people are seldom willing to relinquish their core myths.

The idea of long-lasting, world-shaping global conspiracies is a dangerous projection of personal insecurities and group status loss. But there actually have been conspiratorial cabals focused on specific situations – it is good to expose these secret attempts to distort society for the interests of a few --not all conspiracy theories are paranoid fantasies. Real conspiracies do exist. At every level of society, groups of people regularly get together to plan coordinated action. If they are among the elite, they can powerfully influence particular decisions or even change a society's general direction -- the way we now know that a cabal of bankers pushed for the creation of the Federal Reserve system. But they are usually a response to other forces rather than the initiating trigger – the Federal Reserve was a response to the collapse of the banking system, not the cause. Still, the combination of top-down and bottom-up pressure can really shake things up. In post-WWI Germany, it was the support of major businesses and the old aristocracy that allowed Hitler's insurgent Brown Shirt militias to gain power as a strategy for dislodging the elected Socialists. In our time, it was the funding provided by business leaders seeking market deregulation and tax cuts for the wealthy that let the Trumpites take control of the Republican Party, Congress, and the Presidency.

USING CONNECTIONS

Cynicism rather than paranoia underlies the folk wisdom that "it all depends on who you know" – which, while fatalistic, reflects the reality that relationships cut through society's complexity and open the chance for a serendipitous connection of one's own. From this perspective, access to decision-makers primarily depends on the accidents of birth, on networks of family, church, friendship, workplace, social life, and random acquaintances.

Folk wisdom is correct in understanding that inside connections make a difference. And advocates should not hesitate to use those they have. This is not a substitute for large scale campaigns: people power is the ultimate motor of advocacy success. "Calling your cousin" can sometimes help open doors. Insider politics smacks of arrogance and elitism, but it does occur and furthermore is often, whether we like it or not, a necessary part of the end-stage process of advocacy efforts.

Bottom-Up: Historic Agency

Bottom-up theories of change often embody moral perspectives about human dignity, community, and empowerment. But a strategy based on that theory also needs to be supported by an analysis showing that it will work under the current circumstances, that it will create enough power to push vision into reality. One of the most appealing aspects of traditional Marxism was its belief in the industrial proletariat's inevitable role as the engine of positive social change. The proletariat had "national-historic agency" – they had the need, size, economic role, concentration, self-consciousness, and therefore the power to create an egalitarian and humane new society. It was, for many communists, the certain future of an unstoppable, impersonal, process that inevitably led to a better democratic world – a seductive combination of inside-out and bottom-up theories of change. In fact, for many years, the rising power of working-class movements was a primary driver of change in the industrial world.

Hitching vision to a group with historic agency, with the ability and desire to create change, is part of strategic planning. As the working class in advanced industrial societies became more integrated into reformed social systems, there have been repeated attempts, from many political perspectives, to look for other historical agents. Mao Zedong based his revolution on his belief that anti-colonial nationalist movements would eclipse proletarian revolt as the primary agency of world-scale change. Max Weber saw the development of bureaucracy as the defining dynamic of modern life. Pioneering post-WWII economist Peter Drucker located world-shaping power in the replacement of industrial owner-operators by corporate managers. More recently, Richard Florida said it was the loosely-defined "creative class" that revitalized cities and nations. During the 1960s there were many who elevated Youth as the vanguard agents of change.

AGENCY FROM THE MARGINS

Analyzing social movements from various countries, political scientist Erica Chenoweth believes that agency results not so much from the group's location in the socio-economic system as from its size. Her finding is that non-violent uprisings that engage merely 3.5 percent of the population, and sometimes even less, have repeatedly won society-changing demands. (Violent rebellions have a much lower rate of success.) This kind of analysis underlies people power strategies based on uniting enough of the oppressed, exploited, and marginalized to have sufficient power to catalyze progressive change. The optimism implicit in her writing, from *Why Civil Resistance Works* (2012) to the current *Civil Resistance: What Everyone Needs To Know*, helped inspired the youth-led Sunrise movement's push for climate-saving "mass strikes" and other rebellious outsider strategies.

However, the analysis comes with numerous caveats. The campaign requires active, persistent, visible, and impactful non-compliance – or explicit oppositional action -- by large numbers of people, even when authorities crack down. Not only does the 3.5 percent have to be fully engaged, they have to be at least passively supported by a large proportion of the population. This type of movement is also most effective as a protest against something or as a refusal to participate; it is much easier to build a broad coalition against something everyone hates than to unify people with multiple interests and perspectives around a particular solution. Mass protest is also easier to scale up when directed at particular grievances against a government or other kind of central authority; diffuse targets are harder to explain or focus on. In addition, the success of the non-violent movement often depends on numerous contextual factors beyond the control of the organizers – how brutal is the authority's response? How factionalized is the establishment? Is there supportive international pressure?

And finally, even 3.5 percent is a lot of people. Even restricting the count to adults over age 18, there are about 209 million in the USA population. Three-and-a-half percent is about 730,000 – each of whom needs to be fully committed. Yes, nearly 81 million people voted for Biden, and there were a huge number of committed electoral activists who took advantage of pandemic virtualism to write letters and postcards, to join phone banks, and to contribute money. But for the vast majority of Biden supporters, as political analyst Eitan Hersh points out in *Politics is for Power, How to Move Beyond Political Hobbyism, Take Action, and Make Real Change*, their activism didn't go beyond obsessively watching the news – a form of "cognitive engagement" and an exercise in "partisan cheerleading" that is "more about our own short term emotional and intellectual gratifications.... [than deep] political engagement...."

(It is sobering to point out that Chenoweth's analysis applies to both progressive and fascist uprisings. Nearly 75 million people voted for Trump and while it's impossible to know exactly what percentage of them are hardcore militants, it's just as possible that the 3.5% benchmark was reached on that side as much as Biden's!)

Making the task of activating so many people even more difficult is that we've also learned that education is not a guaranteed path to social or personal behavior change. We've learning that accepting a fact as "true" often depends more on someone's underlying values or religious views, peer group culture, media niche, and leadership modeling. Showing people that they're factually wrong is as likely to make them double-down on their beliefs as to force them to rethink. The collapse of our national culture into media silos and socially-uniform communities, with a reinforcing echo-chamber for every niche, makes changing someone's ideas extremely difficult. (Many people buried in the Fox News and Alt-Right social media echo-chambers sincerely believe that Black Lives Matter and Antifa terrorists are planning to attack their homes.)

And even when people's ideas change, their behaviors often do not. Research reveals that "there's surprisingly little correlation between most people's attitudes and behavior." (Matt Martin, *Fast Company*, 8/03/20) Habits and actions turn out to be primarily shaped by a person's immediate social and physical environment and the larger structural arrangements of their society rather than personal consciousness or will power. Long-term change requires both a changed context and the availability of new ideas that help someone make sense of the situation. A complicated combination.

And yet, this vision of a path through the stultifying weight of established systems and the repressive inertia of traditional culture towards a better future is a necessary inebriant. We need to have hope; we need our hope to be evidence-based and strategically useful.

THE PERPETUAL CIVIL WAR
In America, racism sits at the core of nearly every system. From the nation's founding to today, institutional racism has been

so integral to the economic growth, inter-regional power relationships, control of local elites, and evolving culture of the United States that the recurring struggles of African-Americans for dignity and material improvement has been a major driver of social change. Their centuries-long fight for inclusion, more recently joined by the efforts of other people of color (as well as women, immigrants, and alternative sex/gender adherents), has repeatedly led to society-wide systemic and cultural transformations.

Even so, despite the centrality of their experience and energy for any meaningful progressive movement, African-American do not have the power to succeed on their own – their numbers are too small and their population percentage is shrinking, their economic power too dispersed or marginal. They are the crucial margin of victory as well as the front-line troops for any significant democratic fight. But they require allies to win. It can be done, as shown in Joe Biden's victory over Trump in Southern swing states and the following astounding double Democratic win in the Georgia Senate runoff elections.

The key strategic insight is that, in recent years, while workplace organizing and union mobilization remains important – and vital for workers -- the declining power of unions means that most improvements in both workplace and community well-being have not come from direct economic- or workplace-based efforts. Instead, victories such as the rise in the minimum wage have resulted from political reforms achieved through alliances between liberal and progressive political forces backed by significant levels of grassroots organizing and bolstered by increased non-white turnout. The location of the levers of change has moved.

Even Chaos Has Patterns

Of course, not everything is part of a pattern. In the natural world, the big leaps in evolution are as much about catastrophic events and opportunistic replacements as about the gradual accumulation of accidental mutations. The dinosaurs' disappearance may have been caused by a giant meteor or by massive volcanos, but either way something unique and unprecedented happened and they died, making room for the puny creatures that would unintentionally evolve into us.

Radical disruption can be just as random and powerful in human history – a frigid winter can kill an invading army (Napoleon), a key leader can die (Abraham Lincoln), a new technology can be invented (computers). In economics the restructuring is celebrated as creative destruction, in science as a paradigm shift, in politics as reform or even revolution. Things can emerge out of the blue – but even then, a good analysis of larger forces based on Theories of Change can help you understand what will happen after the dust settles.

10. MAKING SENSE OF CONTEXT:
Weaving Your Way Through Local Reality

What Thackeray invents for the novel is...the way in which history – accidently, fortuitously, calamitously, and unpredictably – enters the...individuals who can only experience it through its particular effects on their private lives.
NICHOLAS DAMES, "INTRODUCTION," VANITY FAIR

When the music changes, so must the dance.
AFRICAN PROVERB

Theories of Change are a macro view of history, about the winds that blow from afar. Context is what you see looking outward from where you are. Context is what shapes "normality" and the political landscape through which we move. A good contextual analysis helps shape strategy, identify allies and form coalitions. Plotting your way through your surroundings allows you to practice the "principled opportunism" that so often creates victory. A grounding in reality also helps you design solutions that will actually solve the problem and survive a later pushback.

There are many ways to dissect and label these interacting societal components and layers. In public health, for example, the jargon name for the multiple concentric circles of influence around us is "socio-ecological," moving outward through Individual, Interpersonal, Community, Organizational, Policy, and Societal. And there are other frameworks; none are more or less correct – just more or less useful to you. Making sense of context requires digging through the preconceptions we bring to a situation, scrupulously examining the data, and re-assembling our view of reality through more useful metaphors. Honest contextual analysis is the basis for successful strategy.

Understanding context is the precondition for finding trends to take advantage of, allies to work with, resources to use, and opposition or obstacles to avoid or pre-empt. In advocacy, with situational knowledge, insightful contextual analysis, and some luck, it is possible to get a good idea about what are the most opportune problems to address and what are the best ways to address them. In order to maximize impact, whether going with the flow or against it, understanding context is the basis for strategic planning.

Of course, the smaller the scope of the changes you seek, the smaller the contextual reality you have to deal with. The bigger the issue, the more that advocacy success is related to what's happening above and around. Advocating for social service benefits for one person may only require understanding the personalities of the people who run an agency's local office. Changing the eligibility rules for a state program requires understanding the fiscal and political situation of the state government department that funds the agency, as well as the legislature's current attitude towards the entire issue. Changing national policies requires understanding not only national economic, demographic, and political dynamics but international forces as well.

Local and national analysis and action are inter-acting. Local action and victories are essential, but they exist inside of the larger patterns that shape our immediate situations and which, if not addressed, will simply keep recreating the particular problem all over again. However, changes at the regional or national level will have the most impact if they create new opportunities for action at the local level; for all the importance of national campaigns, it is at the local level that a base of support is created and sustained. Our greatest impact comes when we choose local issues that embody larger issues – when we find a way to turn a small gear that helps turn a larger one, when we maximize the leverage our limited resources have on impacting larger realities.

I was once the Board Chair of an international solidarity and development organization. One of our programs donated money to rural village women to buy rabbits. A simple thing which both helped them feed their families and earn extra money. Having money of their own also improved the women's status in their patriarchal community. And the increased local supply of food strengthened their village's ability to resist the occupying foreign army around them. It was a wonderful example of how understanding the pressures of a larger context helps generate ideas for small local actions that both provided immediate benefits while contributing to larger dynamics.

While the reality of context is inescapable, our surroundings are at least partially malleable. We are not doomed or pre-ordained. Sometimes it is exactly the "givens" of reality that we feel it's most imperative to try to change –poverty and disease, cruelty and exclusion. Knowing what to demand and how to win those changes requires assessing the context.

Two Metaphors: Stacking Dolls And Atmospheric Layers

It's understandably difficult to see several layers of reality beyond our own. Sometimes metaphors help. Imagine a set of Russian stacking dolls, each nested within the next larger one. Each doll sets a limit for the size and shape of those contained within it -- without mandating exactly what that size and shape must be. Were they alive, the little dolls in the center of the stack would have no idea of the shape or even the existence of the outermost layers, or how they create constraints for the interior space.

We, too, live in the center of multiple constraining social structures and systems. These affect not only ourselves but the entire society, from the economy to our political processes to our culture – shaping the occupational and lifestyle landscapes we inhabit. It therefore also shapes the political and policy choices most people see as possible or impossible, consider desirable or unacceptable, or that they don't even realize exist. It's not surprising that most Americans can barely imagine a successful non-exploitive financial system or a productive but non-hierarchal work place.

However, unlike the nested wooden dolls, the layers of social context aren't static. Each has its own dynamics while simultaneously influencing the others in an endlessly interactive process. So, a second metaphor: Think of the multiple layers of our atmosphere, from the ground to the edge of space, layers of wind and clouds flowing by and into each other, creating low clouds from higher moisture, high winds from low-level heat spots. The changes in one layer can cause significantly new patterns in others. High-level winds – the Jet Stream – can shift, pushing lower clouds into new patterns bringing rain or drought to the land below. And the interaction isn't always incremental, linear, or proximate: chaos theory tells us that a flapping butterfly in China can lead to a tornado in Arkansas. Warm water in the Pacific brings dry winters to New England.

It's true in societal dynamics as well. A banking crisis in Japan can devastate employment levels in East Africa. Contextual change in seemingly remote higher layers can push ground-level reality off into new and sometimes unpredictable directions. A subprime mortgage crisis leads to gun violence and domestic terrorism.

Critical Alliances

Understanding the larger trends is just the first step. Then comes using that understanding to guide your strategies and tactics. The more that the changes you want affect the privileges or power of existing economic, social, institutional, and political hierarchies, the more difficult your fight will be – and the more that your success depends on pushing in roughly the same direction as larger trends. Demographic, technological, climate, and economic trends are like a wind at your back – not sufficient to move you but helpful once you're in motion.

Also critical is taking advantage of divisions within the establishment. Insurgent movements have the greatest chance of winning major structural change when they can ally with dissenting factions of the ruling elites. Serious crises that show the ruling elites to be incapable of maintaining the overall system's stability can provoke serious splits at the top, some portions of which may ally with popular movements creating a force for change bigger than its components. The economic collapse of the 1929 Great Depression discredited corporate leaders and the Republican presidents who so clearly favored them, opening the door to Franklin Roosevelt's reformist wing of the Democratic Party to successful align itself with emerging labor unions, urban ethnic political organizations, and civic movements.

It is also possible for insurgent movements to crack open potential fault-lines in a previously unified upper class. The Civil Rights Movement was built on the endurance, courage, and actions of ordinary people across the South. But the support of the national Democratic Party (however incomplete and inconsistent) was a key factor in its success as well – support that broke apart the long-standing alliance of the national Party with Southern Dixiecrat segregationists. This happened partly because of the national Party's fear that unless it was seen as friendly to civil rights it would lose control of its northern urban base as historically Republican-supporting Southern blacks migrated north.

A campaign is most likely to win both incremental and fundamental change if it aligns both self-interest and moral justification with larger forces in the surrounding society. The push for renewable energy is partly powered by the growing solar-panel industry. #metoo was pushed forward by the growing presence of women in professional and managerial positions. The initial effort to use technology to promote project-based, individualized learning in schools was possible because of the eagerness of the computer industry to expand. This kind of pragmatism involves compromises, which sometimes undermine the moral underpinnings of the effort. But if done strategically – and if everything plays out well – it can provide a way to quickly elevate an idea.

STANDING ALONE

Of course, it's absolutely true that advocacy is about not accepting the world as it is. And there is usually no way to know the limits of the possible without testing them, pushing beyond the borders to see how far you can get no matter what the surrounding context. Sometimes the urgency of an issue pushes people into action even if they know that they are likely to be acting alone or only symbolically. These acts of ethical heroism are the stuff of legends. The people who sailed into nuclear test zones or the Greenpeace efforts to stand between harpooning whale ships and their intended victims – these and others like them set a high bar for what it takes to live out your values.

We can hope that such individual or small group action is an inspirational model for others. Or it just may be what we have to do, like the single person standing in front of the tanks rolling into Tiananmen Square. At other times, you might decide that the situation gives you no choice but to act, even if the context makes success unlikely.

However heroic, martyrdom is a strategy of desperation; it is an extreme over-reliance on volunteerism – the belief that radical social change can be catalyzed at any time through the action of hyper-committed individuals regardless of the larger context. While the hope is that such exemplary action sparks widespread flames, the reaction is as likely to be a clampdown on protest as a general uprising – or the extreme effort may have no effect at all other than the sacrifice of its perpetrators. Che Guevarra's "foco" strategies were a revolutionary version of this, with predictably disastrous results in Bolivia.

Still, under the right circumstances, action at the margins of the political spectrum can set the tone for everyone else; a forced raising of consciousness and of tensions. But individual actions are most potent when there is a parallel mass movement.

The priests and others who poured blood on draft system files in the 1960s were surrounded by a growing draft resistance movement. The Civil Rights movement leaders we now celebrate stood with thousands of African-Americans whose names never appeared in newspapers, who risked or suffered beatings and arrest, or worse, but whose small local acts against segregation gave the Civil Rights Movement its deepest reality in everyday life.

But it is also possible to be so far ahead of the rest of society that you don't attract any attention or provoke any re-evaluation. It is possible to push so uncompromisingly for goals that are so far beyond the limits of current possibility that you end up by yourself with nothing. It is possible to misread the context and tack so directly into the wind that you end up capsizing. The American radicals who split from the Democratic Party in 1948 to form the Progressive Party miscalculated the larger context of the emerging Cold War and ended up isolating New Deal radicals and labor leftists outside the mainstream – one reason for the conservative Republican dominance of the 1950s.

The Future Is Not Inevitable

We are capable of creating our own futures, but we need to understand and deal with the fact that the odds for success increase to the extent we push in parallel to the large-scale forces surrounding us and pick our way through the obstacles in the immediate environment. Changing context starts by acknowledging its presence, analyzing its contours, picking the more promising routes, and being aware of how the lay of the land influences our steps even as we pass through.

I've spent much of the past 15 years working from a public health perspective to promote "active transportation" – walkable and bikeable cities replete with public transportation. In my home state of Massachusetts, we've been phenomenally successful in transforming road design and transportation planning at both the policy and (increasingly) operational level. We worked hard and I'm extremely proud of our accomplishments. But equally important to our success were the shift of young professionals back into cities, the cultural impact of fitness consciousness, the slow realization among city planners that there simply is no room left to build more roads, and the temporary enthusiasm of certain mayors for cycling. Still – I'm willing to celebrate!

Reality is a cloud of possibilities that consolidates upon our interaction with it in the way viewing an electron cloud collapses its infinite locational options into one spot. Reality's solidity is created by the collective actions of the entire population, resulting in the single pathway through time that we call history. But until those actions occur, history doesn't happen and all alternatives are possible.

11. CULTURE, STABILITY, AND CHANGE:

Majoritarian Inertia and Social Tectonics

Our government rests in public opinion. Whoever can change public opinion, can change the government.
ABRAHAM LINCOLN

At any given moment, public opinion is a chaos of superstition, misinformation, and prejudice.
GORE VIDAL

[Culture] is where people make sense of the world, where ideas are introduced, values are inculcated, and emotions are attached to concrete change. Or to put it another way, political change is the final manifestation of cultural shifts that have already occurred.
JEFF CHANG & BRIAN KOMAR, "CULTURE BEFORE POLITICS,"
THE AMERICAN PROSPECT MAGAZINE, JAN/FEB. 2011

We each live in a personal bubble of our unique understanding of the world, shaped by our individual experiences and personality. In contrast, culture is a social process that emerges from the aggregation of the operations of everyday life within a particular society. It is the way we make collective sense of history and current reality. Culture is population-level consciousness and behaviors, shaped by all the events, systems, and trends that our community has lived through. Culture is the lumpy combination of many influences. In the broadest sense, culture is the way a society sees itself and the world.

Individually, we experience ourselves as separate, unique, ourselves. Individually and collectively, we create culture. But we do not live in isolation; our ideas and behaviors are shaped by what came before us and by what we need to do to live in the surrounding socio-economic environment – and each of our external realities are broadly similar to most other peoples'. For all the quickly changing fads and fashions that we adorn ourselves with, societies have relatively homogeneous and stable core cultural themes shared by most of the population. There are, almost always, marginalized groups whose environment is fundamentally different. But that segregation is exactly what makes them marginal, out of the broad mainstream. And, even for them, the surrounding environment permeates and shapes their perception and reality. As James Baldwin wrote about the African-American experience, "We take our shape within and against that cage of reality bequeathed us at our birth."

Culture creates a framework of default ideas and attitudes, with implicit values, that people use to interpret events, often unconsciously. It influences what personal behaviors we see as normal, what types of social relationships we consider desirable, what political and business behaviors we think are legitimate, what kind of future we see for ourselves, and even what kind of life purpose and meaning we seek. Culture shapes our perception of the structures and forces of society, of our context. Culture is as much a part of our surrounding environment and as much shaped by institutional dynamics as the political and economic systems that advocates' strategic analysis usually focuses on.

It is true, as Karl Marx noted nearly 150 years ago, that the ideas of the ruling classes are a society's ruling ideas – not the only ideas, just the dominant ones that set the norms against which all others shape themselves. It's also true that as subordinate sectors of society painfully find ways to win some degree of stability and security within a socio-economic system they don't control, some percentage of them (and many of their organizations) become conservatively tied to the established structures and ideas in order to protect what they've got. As Bernie Sanders painfully learned, a majority of people can support radical change involving many specific issues while resisting any coalescence of their thoughts into a coherent mainstream-rejecting ideological identity. Medicare for all: yes. Socialism: no.

Yet it is also true that cultures are not simply imposed from above. It is also created out of the lives of those below. In fact, in modern times, the commercial drive for ever-new products makes media producers constantly troll the fringes of society for exotica that can be repackaged and sold. But this only works because ordinary people are constantly creating culture that expresses their own needs, hopes, and struggles. Songs, folk tales, dances, clothes styles and slang, even gossip and much more – all go into the mix. The complex cultural mix all this produces both sews people into the status quo and gives them support for resisting it.

Because of its central role and the many ways a society shapes its components to reinforce compliance with its norms, the culture of a stable society is relatively stable. It doesn't radically change. Until it does. And it eventually always does.

Separately Together

Within American society the channels through which our lives flow, our ideas develop, our behaviors are shaped, and our lives play out, are remarkably similar. In most respects the outlines of our lives are within standard-deviation versions of everyone else's story – mass produced by large-scale dynamics affecting millions of others in similar ways. Beyond the superficialities of clothes, food, hobbies, sports-team loyalties, and other visible preferences, almost all our fundamental life choices fall within a narrow range. We are both unique and ordinary. (It is exactly because these small preferences are what distinguish us, and because they are so easily commercially catered to, that fashion and product "personalization" have become such major dimensions of our culture and economy.)

These large-scale patterns of population-wide culture and consciousness are not simple reflections of economic conditions. *New York Times* economics reporter, David Leohardt pointed out that "since 1933...the six presidents who have presided over the fastest job growth have all been Democrats. The four presidents who have presided over the slowest growth have all been Republicans." ("Why Are Republican Presidents So Bad For The Economy?", 2/2/2021). But that hasn't prevented huge numbers of working families from supporting Trump. Paycheck politics is real, but not all powerful.

Societal culture shapes us because, as Wendy Wood, in *Good Habits, Bad Habits*, describes, brain-scan studies show that we mostly and unthinkingly follow the cues and rewards of our immediate and societal surroundings. Conformity is chosen as much as forced upon us. And why not: we are social beings. Most people want to be approved by and fit in with their peers. As social philosopher Eric Hoffer once pointed out, "when people are free to do as they please they usually imitate each other." We take as norms what we assume others, particularly people whom we see as authoritative or admirable in some way, would do in a situation. While this encourages social stability, it makes both individual and population-level change harder.

At the institutional level, "culture trumps policy" was the oft-repeated complaint of a former Massachusetts Secretary of Transportation about his efforts to reform the organizational layers beneath him. He was referring to the way staff did their work based on the past practices that they had been trained to follow and had spent their professional lives becoming comfortable using. The Secretary felt that his staff were only superficially adopting the new attitudes and procedures he was trying to instill.

The engineers' resistance to the Secretary's reforms was also at least partly an expression of the permanent staff's weary experience with the whims of temporary political appointees. But there is some truth to his insight even at the level of society as a whole. Culture makes societies gyroscopic; once in motion they tend to stay upright. This is, to a great degree, because those with wealth, power, and status use their institutional resources -- including laws, violence, economic pressure, and media -- to keep themselves at the thin top. It is also because we are all bathed from birth in cultural messages that make it hard to believe that anything else is possible – and because most people have a stake, no matter how tenuous, in what they've been able to wrest, often with great hardship and effort, from the current situation.

To an amazing extent, we – individually and collectively – are like self-righting sailboats, not only moving in response to winds coming from beyond the horizon but automatically re-aligning ourselves to the pressure when a sudden gust or our own mistakes temporarily turn us over.

Guns And Ideas

Mao Zedong is credited with the slogan that "power comes from the barrel of a gun" (an idea that the National Rifle Association also endorses). And it's obviously true that brute force violence is a trump card with immediate impact. The bully in the playground, the person with the knife, the invading army all get their way. American racism has been enforced by a long series of violent regimes, from slave-catchers to KKK vigilantes to mass incarceration and police killings.

A credible threat of violence can force people to pay attention to the ruler's cultural messages and can even psychologically induce victims to internalize their oppressors' point of view – a sort of "Stockholm Syndrome" of identifying with the dominator as a way out of devastating helplessness. This can be very powerful – a "colonial mindset" still maintained by now-independent former subjects of a foreign country is the bane of the developing world.

However, while shifting the balance of force changes the immediate situation, the victors do not always secure their goals over the long term. Military might wins battles and wars. It is hard to think of anything beyond survival when there is a boot on your throat. But unless it leads to the total collapse of the loser's civilization, force by itself doesn't guarantee long-term control or prevent the next war. Muscle and guns can win control of people's physical reality but not always their minds, can stop public activity but not the myths. Military force can set the stage but doesn't finish the job; that requires shaping culture. Winning the peace is a separate process from winning the war.

Long-term, power comes, most deeply, from shaping a people's perception of reality: what is good or bad about current conditions and what improvements are possible? What are the immediate and background causes of a problem? Is a particular person at fault or is it a more systemic problem? Is the problem caused by institutional malfunction or by the system doing exactly what it is supposed to? What solutions are technically impossible or socially unacceptable? Who has the power to make change?

This deeper understanding of power is expressed in the Black Panther Party's slogan that "power is the ability to define a phenomenon and have it act in a desired manner." What does it take to define the world for entire populations? The "soft imperialism" of having US movies, song, fashions, and language dominate world media was as central to this country's pre-eminence after WWII as its atomic bombs. As a Nigerian TV producer told *The New Yorker* (1/22/18), "Americans don't realize how America-focused the rest of the world is. We get your news; we get your media. We always have to remind ourselves that it's another country." The United States has become the globe's dominant image of prosperity, personal success, and national power. It's what much of the world now wants. (And it is exactly their rejection of this path to the "modern" future that makes today's religious fundamentalists – whether Jewish, Hindu, Buddhist, Muslim, or Christian – so dangerous to US elites.)

Family Projections

Culture, including the consciousness and behaviors it fosters, is shaped by our context. But cultural context does not only reach down to us from our common institutional environment, it also exists in our beginnings within families. Every family is unique. But every newborn – at least every one that survives – has caregivers. Not long ago, I watched my infant grandchild as one adult after another appeared from beyond her visible horizon to pick her up, change her clothes, and move her to a new location. From our beginnings as dependent newborns we are surrounded by people and forces bigger and more powerful than ourselves, over which we have no control and about which we have little understanding as to motives or next moves. Perhaps this primordial experience is why the feeling of being at the mercy of external powers remains so strongly with us through most of our lives.

Similarly, from birth on, we also have a need for order and stability and, eventually, to be able to make sense of the world. As we grow our world expands in complexity. However, as anthropologist Robert Murphy, in *The Body Silent*, writes:

> *The worlds created by the human imagination are far more coherent and structured than the real social systems in which we live, and the mental constructs by which we make sense of society are only loosely related (sometimes inversely) to what is really going on....*

Those "mental constructs" come from our families. We use our families, our first surrounding context and the one whose structure and dynamics have been imprinted within us, as a template for interpreting events and making sense of what's happening around us, of society. As feminism has taught us, family dynamics are our apprenticeship for life. We project the emotional assumptions instilled by our upbringing onto the people and the world around us. Just as much as our expectations about gender relationships, our emotional-political world views are shaped by the family patterns we grew up within. We carry these templates within our hearts and heads; projecting them into our perceptions and opinions about existence and society.

Building on this insight, George Lakoff described how people tend to fall into two groups, partly based on their own upbringing: those with a "strict father model" and those with a "nurturant parent model." Strict father people believe that the world is a dangerous and uncertain place. People need to be tough and self-reliant. There can be no coddling of weaknesses. Rules must be harshly enforcement. Strong, unyielding leadership is necessary, hierarchy is inevitable. Outsiders cannot be trusted. Nurturing parents believe in helping rather than punishing, prefer negotiation to violence, and think the more fortunate should help strangers in need.

These deep-seated beliefs shape the way we interpret and understand the world, which affects our beliefs about what is possible and what is good, and therefore what we try to accomplish and what we do in the world. It shouldn't be surprising that one of Lakoff's groups ends up supporting Trump and the other joins the women's' march.

Limits Of Education

Recent research suggests that we – people in general – tend to filter the stream of information flowing towards us to reduce the attention we pay to anything that contradicts our existing assumptions, biases, and beliefs. And if something that challenges our world view does get through, we react by becoming even more committed to our original position. Even exposure to someone else's reality, "walking a mile in their shoes" or living in a new place, simply opens the possibility of reconsideration but by itself doesn't necessarily change someone's underlying perspective, framework of understanding the world, or default assumptions and opinions. People respond more to what pushes their emotional buttons than what tries to convince their logical mind – a psychological reality that is the basis for the entire modern advertising industry.

The process is even more pronounced when we are with like-minded others: group confirmation amplifies people's initial inclinations, pro or con, on any particular issue. And we are increasingly living in echo chambers of like-minded reinforcement. Mass media and the digital world have been restructured, from news to entertainment, into hundreds of distinct niche channels designed to attract separate audiences that seldom overlap or interact. Even beyond our continuing patterns of racial and wealth separation, we are increasingly living in more culturally and ideologically homogeneous patterns. Bill Bishop, in *The Big Sort*, shows that as people move around for work or other reasons, they relocate themselves near churches, cafes, life-style opportunities, racial/ethnic mixes, and other factors that reflect their culture and values. Combined with the increasingly ideologically based gerrymandering of our political jurisdictional boundaries, people have infrequent personal contact with any alternative to their current beliefs and lifestyles. And then the pattern sticks: the vast majority of people inherit their party loyalties. In times of stability, the children of Democrats and Republicans typically vote as their parents did.

Even so, most of us carry around a mishmash of inherited loyalties, peer influences, often unconscious biases, random factoids, snippets of logic, and personal experiences. Few people's world view solidifies into a coherent and consistent ideology. People's evaluation of politicians is generally based on the person's emotional appeal and symbolic positioning – George Bush was famous for being someone "you could go out for a beer with." And yet, jumbled as it is, we hold on to our perspective, using it to filter input, make decisions, and take action.

> *[It] is a necessary feature of cognition...So much information pours into the mind, ranging from sensory experience to discursive and mediated inputs of all kinds, that some kind of personal organizing system is necessary to make sense of things in ways that allow one to decide and to act.* (The Ministry for the Future, Kim Stanley Robinson)

Stability Works

Most people enjoy challenges, but few of us want to abandon everything we have and are. In the late 1970s, writer Ellen

Goodman researched how feminism had changed what people wanted from family relationships. As she explained in *Turning Points*, the vast majority wanted change but not too much disruption; they wanted improvements but not too much upset; meaningful challenge but with a safety net of stability. People want to look forward to a better future without losing too much of the past. We want to grow, not be reinvented.

One result of our personal life-choice caution and our collective social inertia is that most of us go along with society's default daily behavior patterns most of the time. It's not that we're lazy; it's just that very few of those actions seem to involve very important value judgements. Why not just go with the flow, even if it means we never climb over the steep river banks to experience the wider world? That unseen terrain is unknown, uncertain, possibly unsafe, and hard to imagine. In any case, there are simply too many decisions in each day to completely think through the implications of every little thing we do. MRI scans tracking brain activity indicate that up to 43% of our behaviors are habitual and unconscious ("The Resistance," *The New Yorker*, 10/28/19).

Even when we turn against the current, the deviations from normal we generally take are relatively small – we may recycle instead of dispose, eat local organics rather than junk foods, buy "fair trade" clothes instead of sweat shop products, or ride a bike instead of take a car. But we don't leave. And these individual actions, by themselves, do little to destabilize society's overall dynamics and hierarchies.

Furthermore, there is a functionally useful aspect to our overall conformity: no matter how unsatisfactory the status quo, we have learned to manage it. Stability is protective: change brings the unknown and uncertain, full of potential risks to whatever is currently enjoyed. For all our complaints about the way things are, most people are able to create a sufficiently satisfactory personal life within the limits of the socially acceptable – a life, no matter how bounded, replete with a full complement of personal growth, moral triumphs, and love. No matter how bad our situation, we tend to hold on to it. Harriet Tubman – runaway slave, abolitionist, and women's rights advocate – who risked her life multiple times to bring other slaves North, supposedly said that "I could have saved thousands if only they knew they were slaves." We live and life goes on.

Persistence Of The Past

Shaking loose from the drag of old cultural patterns is hard, even when people fight for something better. Our current culture helps shape the type of political action we are willing to take and the type of society we fight for when crisis creates the opportunity. So what we end up with is never entirely new. Even though each transition creates new realities, it also (sometimes unknowingly) incorporates old patterns. We never fully leave the past behind.

The Civil War wiped out the world of the slave plantation, but didn't eliminate the effects of slavery on either whites or black people. Women's suffrage began the process of freeing females from being the legal wards of their male protectors, but didn't end patriarchy or most women's accommodation to a subordinate role. Even as many anti-Vietnam War protesters became increasingly radicalized by the continuing US violence, they continued to embody traditional patterns in other areas – from gender roles to social class hierarchies – leading to a "women's revolt" within the anti-war movement.

Even when history seems to jump, we walk towards the future with our heads and hearts still located in the past. Like plants, social change movements – no matter how utopian or revolutionary – draw their nourishment from the ground they grow out of and bring much of it with them. The past endures even when everything changes. Advocates and organizers should never stake their entire strategy on total change. Perfection is neither attainable nor, probably, even desirable either as a goal or as a result. As Margaret Mead pointed out, "Were the world we dream of attained, members of that new world would be so different from ourselves that they would no longer value it in the same terms in which we now desire it. We would no longer be at home in such a world."

Loosening The Binding Ties

At the individual level, behavioral change is hard – as evidenced by all the jokes about failed New Year's Resolutions. Will power is not enough. Similarly, at the societal level, it is hard to escape the glued grasp of culture. It is hard to shake off the past. But it is exactly because culture emerges from the operations of everyday life, that change does happen, that culture does shift. Sometimes it happens in one gigantic flip. Usually, however, that tipping point is preceded by a slow accumulation of smaller building blocks.

As the large-scale drivers of change force the structures of society to evolve, the culture gets stressed. The pressures build up slowly, often with fringe cultural expressions as advance indicators. Overall, things may remain static until some trigger moves entire sectors of the population into a new cultural position. And suddenly, everything is different. Nothing changes; until it does. Large numbers of "ordinary" people do shift their deepest, sometimes even unconscious, assumptions about human nature and social dynamics. And they change behaviors.

While advocacy groups grow one person at a time because of individual challenges and needs, large-scale shifts in social norms and political loyalties happen to hundreds of thousands or millions of people at roughly the same time. And significant population-scale changes in world view and political loyalties do occasionally occur, including gut feelings about the way society is governed and who are appropriate governors. What changes our collective minds?

Population-Scale Change

Individually, we are generally most open to change at un-anchored periods of life transitions. Adolescence, going away to college, marriage, work, or the desire for upward mobility may move someone into a new environment that encourages, if not assumes, conformity to a different set of norms. Or, most dramatically, a person's old life may be ripped apart by some traumatic dislocation such as divorce, physical or mental illness, death, occupational problems, violence, war, or large-scale eco-nomic collapse – or by insidious long-term stresses such as ra-cism and poverty.

Like the shifting of tectonite plates that cause earthquakes, large-scale society-level cultural shifts are not frequent. Not sur-prisingly, large numbers of people are most open to new ideas during times of large-scale crisis and transition. People look for alternatives when their society experiences systemic fail-ures or disruptive changes – climate, technology, war, depres-sion – which significantly reduce the ability of existing elites to maintain the established order and people are no longer able to meet their basic needs. The status quo is no longer working. Sometimes, the collapse happens suddenly. The collapse of the military dictatorships in Greece and Argentina following their battlefield defeats in Cyprus and the Falkland Islands are good examples. In a parallel to the Chinese idea of the Mandate of Heaven, those nations' established political systems fell because they lost the primary legitimizing reason for their authority.

Often, however, these structural changes develop slowly, setting in motion changes in people's lives that eventually get expressed in their culture. The migration of Southern African-Americans freed them of the enormous weight of Jim Crow vigilantes and led to an outpouring of music, writing, and art. The post-WWII move of returning soldiers of European descent from their par-ents' urban ethnic ghettos to the suburbs – aided by cheap GI mortgages and expanding highways – helped cement their tran-sition from Italian, Irish, Polish, and Jewish into "white." The movement of mid-west manufacturing to the American South to overseas turned the Rust Belt into an employment wasteland and fostered an inward-looking anger at established elites. The emergence of higher education–requiring professional and technical work as the most desirable job sectors left working class kids stuck in poor schools and few options, contributing to the current opioid epidemic.

These structural changes are often facilitated and accelerated by new technologies. Long before computers, the development of the cotton gin, steam engine, electrical generator, internal combustion engine, and other technologies shook up their societies. These disruptions forced radical change in the ways people had previously earned a living, their families were structured, the level of security and safety they felt, and the way the surrounding society functioned. Advocates who see these types of trends coming can begin defining issues and connecting to constituencies in ways that help victims avoid purely reactionary defensiveness in favor of more systemic understandings and forward-looking solutions

TRIGGERS

Bill Moyer's "*History is a Weapon: The Movement Action Plan*" manifesto points out that social change ideas percolate through society in often invisible ways. Just because mainstream media and politicians are not discussing an issue does not mean that the ground isn't shifting. But public awareness and concern seldom reach critical mass until some triggering event, a crisis or failure of business of the established order, brings the background changes visibly forward. FDR's New Deal, based on a new coalition of labor, urban ethnics, Southern populists, and middle-class small business families, was only politically possible because the Great Depression had dramatically discredited the business establishment and their ruling Republican allies. The United States elected its first non-white president in 2008 partly because the election came just as Wall Street's speculative housing bubble was bursting.

Then and now, people respond by finding new ways to make sense of their lives and understand the world around them. In the early 1800s the shift from farming to industry depopulated and depressed rural areas and threw people into crowded cities – which sparked huge religious revival movements, a "back to nature" health food movement (Graham Crackers were invented then), as well as Transcendentalism, utopian communities, new literary and artistic forms, and massive political movements of both radical and conservative hues. The 2016 presidential election's elevation of non-establishment fringe candidates and their ability to mobilize huge numbers of voters suggests that we are in the middle of similarly profound domestic and even international structural adjustments.

RELIGIOUS CONTRADICTIONS

Religion sits right in the middle of cultures' contradictions. The translation, through culture, from social context into personal perception is driven at the deepest levels by the fact that humans are meaning-creating and purpose-needing creatures. We create stories, or myths, to explain the world and help us deal emotionally and intellectually with that before which we are most helpless: nature, death, and the accidents of our lives. Religion is the primary embodiment of this, although secular myths also help explain our place in the world, our connections with others.

The deep human need for transcendence – a way to believe that our lives have purpose and value larger and longer than ourselves or our daily routines – creates a powerful interplay between political movements and religious revivals. Organized religion tends towards the conservative, if not further right.

> *Whether consciously or not (and in most cases not), [the] worldview...[of] ordinary citizens ... rests on presumptions that originate in [their] religious thinking...[Historically,] religious institutions filled a dual role: circumscribing individual behavior so as to enable people to live together amicably, and providing for the material needs of those who for one reason*

or another failed to provide for themselves—in both cases, so
that government would not have to do so....[Even today,] reli-
giously committed Americans of nearly all faiths see less need
for government services and government intervention than do
most citizens of other high-income countries. In conjunction
with the far greater share of Americans who identify with one
or another religion, and who participate in church services
and other religious activities, the implication... is profound....
Among evangelicals who stand to benefit most from various
forms of government regulation, many are nonetheless op-
posed to it.... (Religion and the Rise of Capitalism, Benjamin Friedman)

But religious ethics of caring for others, interpersonal dignity, moral motivations can also have societal implications. And when people believe that it is possible to create a better world in the here-and-now they tend to join political movements. When those movements fail to provide the degree of social and personal change or the level of emotional coherence and spiritual satisfaction people are seeking – when the movements collapse or even when they win and then cease to inspire – people then turn (back) to religion, which provides not only a guide for life but a promise of survival afterwards. Then, eventually, as the fundamentalist energy that fueled the revival turns into repressive cultural heavy-handedness, or as religious energy becomes ossified in institutionalized hierarchies, and when the opportunity for this-world improvements appears real, people turn again to more secular politics.

The Great Awakening of the 1730s and 40s helped lay the groundwork for the American Revolution two decades later; the dissolution of the Revolution's idealism into sectional and class conflict led to the Second Great Awakening of the early 1800s... which fed into the rise of Abolitionism in the 1840s and so on. Similarly, during the 1950s through the 1970s, the world's yearnings were expressed in a range of progressive, secular political movements: anti-colonial and national liberation movements, anti-apartheid and Civil Rights struggles, anti-war and youthful countercultural movements, Women's and Gay movements. It was no accident that as many of those movements crested and declined in the 1980s and 90s, they were replaced by growing religious fundamentalism around the world. And someday the pendulum will swing again.

It should not be surprising that religious movements arise during periods of social stress; or that they almost always have the contradictory combination of backward-looking reaction with status-quo challenging bottom-empowerment. Politics and religion flow into each other, feed one another, and compete with each other.

Change Within Stability

Like particles obeying Newton's First Law of Inertia, we humans tend to keep doing what we've always done until pushed to change by something outside ourselves. When a society is functional and stable people tend to acquiesce; to go with the flow. We generally accept the people in power and the current hierarchies as "what is" even if imperfect. People want to be able to feed their family, to realize at least some of their hopes and expectations, and to feel safe. However, when these conditions fail, when the rulers seem unable to manage things well enough to allow people to meet their needs, and if people have been exposed to an idea of a viable alternative, then rebellion becomes possible.

In our media-saturated and technologically innovative age, large-scale cultural change is probably going to occur more frequently than in the slower-moving past. And once a seismic-level political change occurs, and if it gets institutionalized in new organizations and policy structures, it can be very enduring. Enrique Penalosa, former mayor of Bogota, Colombia, has pointed out that the complexity and disjointed nature of the United States' political system makes change happen slowly, but once something is done it's equally hard to reverse. There is a similar truth about cultural change.

Even though nothing seems to change most of the time, even when there are long periods between major upheavals (and even between moments of minor reform), the tectonic plates beneath our everyday rituals are on the move, building tensions that will eventually be released. The fundamental dynamics of human history continue to churn even during periods of political quiet. Like the tides, mass movements and periods of history rise and ebb. Today, as the cultural backlash against modernity escalates around the world, and the rising right wing within the US gives money and corporations more power over people, we need to find the remaining and emerging new sources of power rising from our human cores, which allow us to continue working for progressive change. The wheel will turn.

SECTION V:
STRATEGIC ISSUES

Election days come and go. But the struggle of the people to create a government which represents all of us and not just the one percent – a government based on the principles of economic, social, racial and environmental justice – that struggle continues.

BERNIE SANDERS

12. FOUNDATIONAL VISIONS:
Community, Equality, Freedom, Democracy

13. WHY THE PUBLIC SECTOR CAN'T BE RUN LIKE A BUSINESS:
Universal, Democratic, Open-Ended

14. PUBLIC-PRIVATE PARTNERSHIPS:
Creating Public Value through Privatizing, Outsourcing, and Collaboration

12. FOUNDATIONAL VISIONS:
Community, Equality, Freedom, Democracy

Utopia is impossible to achieve but essential to believe in.
ANONYMOUS

The true test of a religion or ideology or any group is how it perceives and treats non-members.
ALSO ANONYMOUS

Strategic planning starts with vision – your description of the better future that your mission is to help create. However, vision is not enough. Vision is only wishful fantasy without analysis – a description of current reality done in ways that reveal a path to sustainable achievement. Still, knowing what you are trying to achieve makes it easier to focus your effort. As the Wonderland caterpillar told Alice, the direction you should go depends on where you want to arrive.

Vision is most inspiring, useful, and powerful when it is broad, open-ended, and expresses core values and ideals. It has to be sufficiently inviting and flexible enough to be relevant to more than a narrow range of true believers. At the same time, it needs to be concrete enough to serve as the launching pad for general strategies and specific goals.

As one starting point, Frances Moore Lappé, whose *Diet For A Small Planet*, helped reframe public consciousness around the interconnections of nutrition, agriculture, and the environment, bases her political thinking on the three "states of being" that humans need to thrive: personal agency to know that our voices count, meaning based on a sense of purpose beyond our own survival, and connection in communities of common purpose. She believes that these are the basis for personal and interpersonal dignity, which is the ultimate promise of democracy, "humanity's only positive vision of governance." Which leads to her strategic goals of fighting for "First, inclusive, distributed power. Second, transparency to keep power accountable to the 'general welfare'... Third...a culture of mutual accountability."

Vision should always hang a little beyond pragmatic possibility without becoming unbelievable. It needs to be a beckoning dream, one of those "utopian fantasies that had always been necessary to inspire people to the passion and self-sacrifice required to actually work to transform the world in the direction of greater freedom and greater equality" (David Graeber, *Direct Action: An Ethnography*).

Vision not only shapes an advocacy group's activity. It is also vital for explaining the group and its goals to the surrounding society. To do that, vision must be perceived as "legitimate" – meaning that it must have some connection to the surrounding society's professed values, cultural trends, and political history.

American Context: Liberty Uber Alles

It is impossible to build a successful movement in America based on anti-Americanism. While we can learn from people around the world, fortunately this nation's heritage is sufficiently multi-threaded to include much for progressives to build on. In addition to inspiring stories of struggle, it's vital that the political principles emerging from the American Revolution were expressed in universal terms: "inalienable rights", "We the People", "life, liberty, and the pursuit of happiness." Some of the revolutionaries took these statements literally, subscribing to the radical egalitarianism of Tom Paine's "Common Sense." The explosive implications of these ideals have inspired people ever since.

Of course, there were other threads. Most of the leaders of what could more properly be called our civil war with Britain had more conservative goals. While the Founding Fathers' rejection of monarchy was history-making, their functional goal was to use national independence to limit the power of government over their commercial activity. They were not interested in unleashing a radical overturning of domestic hierarchies. The liberty they sought was only their own. Their use of universal language simply expressed their belief that they – white, male, propertied – embodied the legal presence of everyone else. The constitution they wrote limited the democratic impact of universal ideals by allowing slavery and the legal dominance of men over women. Jefferson owned other humans; Hamilton fought general suffrage. But they saw no contradiction between their idealist words and their hierarchal reality – in their minds, they were "the people."

Today's conservatives, libertarians, and "original intent" constitutionalists are the inheritors of historic liberalism's originally democratic vision of competitive private markets as the antidote to centralized monarchal dictatorship. In the name of individual liberty, they reject both government (public) regulation of property as well as egalitarianism of any type. In their view, civilization is based on the ability of property owners to do what they want with their assets with the least possible constraints. Although they don't think of themselves this way, their demand for unlimited personal autonomy and the primacy of property rights is a form of capitalist anarchism.

Their economic anarchism is contradicted by their political authoritarianism. They have no doubt that being rich and powerful is sufficient proof of their superior fitness and their right to run society as they believe necessary. Like the Founding Fathers, they believe that the general good is expressed in and created by their own success. What's good for them is good for everyone. But this projection of self-interest on national policy requires them to seek constraints on political democracy – if democracy were to prevail, those with less resources have historically proven themselves prone to use government to impose "discriminatory taxes" on the wealthy.

Ultimately, the market-libertarian position rests on a belief that individuals do not have any non-voluntarily chosen or non-contractually described responsibility to anyone else. Tea Party libertarians were at least honest about where they were coming from with their slogan that "you are not entitled to what I earn" and the statement that sick people without their own health insurance should be allowed to die. Mitt Romney's Presidential campaign speeches about the need to choose between an "Entitlement Society or an Opportunity Society" is a slicker, but no less slippery, move in the same direction. The most explicit description was British Prime Minister Margaret Thatcher's statement that "there is no such thing as society: there are individual men and women, and there are families."

Just as powerfully, America's decentralized frontier history and the slow, fragmented assembly of our multi-ethnic population has created a cultural individualism to match our anti–central government political origins. Even the 1960s anti-establishment's countercultural slogan, "do your own thing," can be seen as a libertarian demand for individual liberty. From 1776 until today, visions of liberty have been entwined with American nationalism as expressed in the revolutionary-era slogans still chanted by Trumpite conspiracy-fighting insurrectionists: "Don't Tread On Me" and "Live Free or Die."

Reclaiming Democratic Universalisms

Fortunately, American history has equally rebellious but more progressive threads expressed in the history of resistance to slavery, workplace exploitation, government repression, social and cultural oppression. We can also domesticate the positive visions created by other revolutionary movements that pushed beyond the American fight for national independence. The French Revolution expanded the scope to "Liberté, égalité, fraternité" – pushing past the political sphere to include social and community relationships. (And the wonderful feminist twist: "Liberté, égalité, maternité".) Socialism moved the equalitarian vision of democracy into the economic sphere. And the repeatedly recurring ethical themes of most religions are valuable ingredients: honesty, charity, respect for the reflection of the divine in each of us, self-awareness, kindness to strangers – even to the point of the biblical injunction to demand from each according to their ability, give to each according to their needs (*Acts*, 4:34-35). These enlargements of what a better future might look like are essential parts of what shapes progressive visions today. However, advocates still need a way to succinctly and powerfully express these values and ideals in American terms, in language appropriate to our own culture and traditions.

We need to combine all this into visions that emphasize the positive connections between people, our fundamental similarity in needs and worth, and our right to live our own lives within a context of mutual aid and social responsibility. We need visions that are rich enough to encompass our variations and universal enough to unite us, concrete enough to provide guidance and radical enough to inspire action, common enough to be understandable and hopeful enough to pull us forward.

A good starting point are the ideals of community, equality, freedom, and democracy. Each is rich with implications. Each emerges from known themes of American history -- which also means that each contains enough internal complications to require active balancing among its own threads and with the other three.

Community

The hole at the bottom of American individualism is personal isolation. Despite our mythologizing of the frontier hero single-handedly (and often violently) solving problems before riding off alone, few of us would welcome a totally solitary life. Because of our physical and emotional inability to survive without each other from conception to death, community is inescapable. Our need and drive to connect is one of the most primal and powerful forces shaping human existence. Community is a key goal of the entire spectrum of connections starting with family then expanding to ethnicity, religion, tribe, and nation.

Because we cannot survive on our own, because we grow stronger when encouraged and supported, evolution has shaped us to reach out. And the drive for connection is expansionist, so we reach out past the original infant-mother bond into our surrounding family and then into the larger networks of friends, colleagues, neighbors, co-religionists, and more. Community, at its best, emerges from shared experience and manifests as solidarity and mutual aid. At its worst, community leads to exclusion and even violence against the "outsider," the "alien," the "Other."

Humans aren't inherently either good or bad. We simply start with a set of inborn drives: to eat, to stay warm, to connect with others, and to empower ourselves to achieve these needs. We have innumerable individualizing neonatal characteristics from genes, uterine conditions, and our mother's life during pregnancy. But we become who we are as those initial ingredients interact and develop because of how our surroundings – from family structure and culture to the accidents of location and history – shape the ways that we are able to express, develop, and satisfy those innate drives.

Even more: feminist theory teaches us that family dynamics shape society as a whole. The family shapes our deepest assumptions about interpersonal relations, gender and social hierarchies, and the nurturing or dangerousness of the outside world. We spend our lives living out and dealing with those powerfully formative lessons. And we build social systems and societies that embody those assumptions.

From birth on, humans are social creations. If ignored we will not grow; if left alone we will die. "A human being becomes human not through the casual convergence of certain biological conditions but through an act of will and love on the part of other people," points out Italo Calvino. Our commonality, our membership in the human family, is expressed through our innate need, desire, and drive for connection – for community.

For progressive advocates, helping facilitate respectful and mutually supportive connections – building community – is both a strategic goal and an internal organizational necessity.

We work for love and acceptance if not esteem in our family, among our peers, and within our communities. Family ties merge into tribal connections and these evolve into religious, racial, and national identities. Sometimes, these overlap peacefully, reinforcing the most empathetic, compassionate, and cooperative elements of each. Sometimes one of them gets mobilized into an exclusionary and aggressive community willing to use "our" power to benefit ourselves at the Others' expense.

This is all done, of course, in the name of our group's most positive values and in order to defend against "unprovoked" attacks. As Alexander Solzhenitsyn wrote, "To do evil a human being must first of all believe that what he's doing is good, or else that it's a well-considered act in conformity with natural law."

Us And Them

Communities emerge from the group bonds people build based on a common identity, time spent in a shared condition, or on shared interests. Being part of a community engenders a feeling of connection to the group as a whole and a certain degree of loyalty to organizations, programs, or activities linked to the group. Community is a group-creating process rather than an atomizing or individualizing one. And, yet, almost inevitably, communities are defined by boundaries: a distinction between "us" and "them" turning non-members into outsiders and "the Other."

Sometimes, the separation is imposed from outside. When a group is segregated from the surrounding society, its members tend to – and sometimes have no choice except to – turn inward, as did former slaves in America and Jews in pre-WWII Eastern Europe. This can allow a vibrant internal culture and economy to develop, as community members have no choice but to socialize with each other and buy from their own. Sometimes this serves as a basis for self-definition, for turning rejection and denigration into solidarity and pride. It is one of the engines of today's identity politics. Black pride, feminism, non-binary gender identity, anti-colonial nationalism, Zionism -- are all, at least partly, efforts to turn negative definitions and treatment into a source of strength.

Sometimes the separation is enacted through cultural denigration or social mistreatment rather than physical segregation. Nonetheless, like explicit violence, this also creates a negative emotional spectrum from embarrassment to fury, from hurt to despair, from internalized self-deprivation to projected hate. People who are overwhelmed by their situation, who feel hopeless and even incapable of anger, can also become self-destructive – one cause of the alcoholism, drug addiction, and suicide in non-white and indigenous communities, and even in the hollowed-out rust belt communities of the American Midwest.

> *Vanishing jobs, disintegrating families and other social stressors had unleashed a rising tide of fatal despair ...From 1999 to 2013 [in the United States] mortality had risen sharply... because white working-class people ages 45-54 were drinking themselves to death with alcohol, accidentally overdosing on opioids and other drugs, and intentionally killing themselves, often by shooting or hanging. ...This disturbing trend mirrored what had previously occurred among inner-city Black people in the 1970s and 1980s.... [when] Black victims of crack cocaine and the AIDS epidemic represented an early wave of deaths of despair....* "It's Time To Define Despair and Its Risks", by Bruce Bower, Science News, 1/30/2021*

EXTENDED FAMILIES

The two most important things about relatives, my mother used to say, are that you don't get to choose them and that they take care of one another. Back in the day, when most families were extended and lived together, you simply accepted that Uncle Al was loud, that Aunt Sarah was obnoxious, that Cousin Bob told bad jokes, and that each of the other people in the house were just who they were. It was a small classroom for learning to tolerate differences, a lesson that could be generalized.

But today's families are nuclear. Today, we have to consciously work to create places where different kinds of people mingle across racial or social class or religious lines. We have to re-learn how to accept others as peers and as a legitimate part of our own lives and public activity. The more malleable the defining characteristic of a community, the more inclusive and open it tends to be. Neighborhood-based and workplace-based communities can encompass anyone who lives or works there. Communities that emerge out of a group's shared struggle to join the social mainstream tend to be relatively open to whoever is willing to join the fight.

All this is still aspirational, visionary. A recent poll from PRRI/ The Atlantic finds that at least 20% of respondents almost never intermingle with anyone of a different race and almost one-third have little or no contact with anyone of a different sexual orientation. Advocates need to build inclusive communities within their organizations and campaigns. But they also need to make increasing inclusion a central theme of their demands for societal change. Creating an inclusive society requires learning, as President Obama said, that we're all in this together.

Equality

Equality, at its best, gives everyone a solid foundation of resources, rights, and opportunity to develop any talent or interest; to be able to access and utilize all that society has; to be treated with dignity and respect; to go anywhere and interact with anyone – regardless of wealth, race, gender, skin color, age, disability, national origin, belief. Equality is the basis for democracy. At its worst, the idea of equality is a fake-front façade used to hide a society's structural inequalities. Professor Michael Sandel, in "*The Tyranny of Merit*" describes the "meritocratic hubris of the successful" as the sincere conviction by those who land on top that their success is primarily due to their own effort and worth, rather than a less self-affirming story that it was their ability to make the most of where their family history inserted them into the world.

FOUR METAPHORS

Imagine a steeply tilted playing field on which certain groups are forced to compete. Among the team starting at the bottom are a few extraordinary individuals who are occasionally able to score despite the imposed handicap. But it shouldn't be surprising that most of that team's players find that the incline too great to surmount no matter how hard they try. Even when taking age, gender, education, and region into account, Black workers on average are paid nearly 15% less than white workers. The fact is that group discrimination prevents all but the most extraordinary individuals from having a fair chance to succeed; that the elimination of that bias will allow each person to achieve according to their individual ability.

Now imagine a group of people trying to look over a fence at a baseball game. They are all free to come to the fence – that is equality of opportunity, there is no formal discrimination. But the shorter people are still not able to see anything – unless they also have something to stand on. The point is that equality of opportunity is not the same as equity, which goes beyond formal rights to encompass the range of supports needed for individuals – or groups -- to make use of the opportunity. Succeeding in school or a job or homeownership or anything else requires having other kinds of support beyond non-discriminatory acceptance letters allowing you to show up – transportation that doesn't assume car ownership; child care that doesn't assume available babysitters (much less full-time nannies), encouragement and respect responsive to the pain of previous rejection, the chance to fail and try again.

Still, what even the fence-overlooking metaphor leaves out is the underlying fact that the inequities needing correction are not created by something inherent to the person, such as their height, but about the discriminatory patterns in the surrounding society. The support needed has societal causes such as training to make up for having been only able to attend inferior schools; introductions to employers to make up for a lack of connection with people able to make a referral. For this, the better metaphor is a bonsai plant which is small not because of its genetic history but because of the stunting size of the pot it is kept in and the disabling way it is repeatedly cut off from its roots.

But what all three of those images leave out is that disadvantage is cumulative over generations. We need a fourth image: Like water flowing through a series of leaking ponds, each move reduces the amount of resources available for fish in the next pond down. Lower-income families do not inherit and are unable to accumulate the surplus resources – time, energy, savings, property, connections – that allow them to deal with setbacks and take advantage of opportunities while managing daily life. This is true for people of all races. But it's most concentrated among minorities. According to the Brookings Institute, in 2019 the median wealth of a typical white household was $188,200 -- nearly 8 times the $24,100 held by the typical Black household. Past discrimination against African-Americans for housing, education, and jobs not only hurts those immediately affected but puts their children and grandchildren in a deepening hole compared with the larger society. The average Black household headed by someone with an advanced degree has less wealth than a white household headed by someone with only a high-school diploma.

These multi-generational effects can have a cultural expression in what Lakota sociologist Maria Yellow Horse Brave Heart describes as "historical unresolved grief" – the past brutalities that traumatized communities that led to today's depression, suicide, addition, even child and domestic abuse as well as to continuing struggles for dignity, justice, and well-being.

EQUITY IN MOTION

These patterns of historic personal and institutional discrimination, and their multi-generational systemic effect, are exacerbated by the inherent effect of markets to increase inequality, to
redistribute wealth upwards to those best positioned to exploit
opportunity and extract profit. For equity to be systematic,
every program and policy needs to incorporate an awareness
that there is no such thing as being "wealth neutral" – like drop-
ping a ball on a hill, the impact of a program or policy will roll
down the existing tilt in power and resources unless explicitly
designed to move the other way.

Equity is important not merely as a value in its own right, but
because wealth inequity is a significantly contributing factor in
so many of society's problems. Richard Wilkinson and Kate Pickett's important book, *The Spirit Level*, summarized the research
as showing that

> *[health and social] problems in rich countries are not caused
> by the society not being rich enough (or even by being too rich),
> but by the scale of material differences between people within
> each society being too big…. Greater equality, as well as im-
> proving the wellbeing of the whole population, is also the key
> to national standards of achievement and how countries per-
> form in lots of different fields.*

Equality on a societal scale requires universal systems that provide a relatively secure and high quality of life baseline for
everyone – sufficient health care, education, housing, food, cultural and recreational activity, and more. Programs need to be
universally available and affordable, or at least available to a
broad swath of the population, because programs intended only
for poor people almost always end up as poor programs without
influential constituencies to demand their improvement. The
decline of public housing as it changed from a WWII veterans'
benefit to a poor house is a prime example. This is not a "nanny
state" smothering of individuality. It is about eliminating the
holes of misery into which a market-based economy allows

people to fall.

GOOD FROM BOTTOM TO TOP

Equality is not only important for those located on the lower rungs of the income ladder. Inequality undermines an entire society, economically, politically, and even in the personal well-being of those at the top. It's true that, to an extent, inequality helps drive various kinds of positive activity as people strive to climb upward, or simply to survive. But when the tilt gets too steep a society ends up undermining the very conditions that make prosperity possible. Summarizing recent research about inequity, Atossa Araxia Abrahamian writes in *The Nation* (10/8/18):

> ...*extreme disparities [are] harmful because they lead to abuses of power and structural barriers to prosperity, as well as the social tensions and reactionary political movements that follow.... The imbalance, in other words, distorts society as a whole, creating a host of social ills that could ultimately threaten capitalism itself.*

Interestingly, there is mounting evidence that the bigger the gap between the rich and the poor, and the more that the world seems like a jungle of all against all, the more insecure even the powerful feel and the more stress corrodes their personal lives. Similarly, Wilkinson and Pickett write:

> *The assumption is that greater equality [only] helps those at the bottom.... The truth is that the vast majority of the population is harmed by greater inequality.... [The data shows that] greater equality brings substantial gains [in health and social wellbeing] even in the top occupational class and among the richest or best-educated quarter or third of the population...People at almost all income levels, not just the poor...do worse in more unequal societies.*

WEALTH AND RESPECT

All this implies the need for a drastic narrowing of the space between the bottom and top levels of living conditions, incomes, and wealth. However, it doesn't require absolute sameness in outcomes or resources. It doesn't require that everyone impacted in any way by any decision has equal power in decision-making. Nor does it require the elimination of all hierarchies in professional or civic life. Every society in history has had – and every one in the future will inevitably have -- some differentiations in wealth, power, status, and upward mobility. But the presence of a short ladder with easily grasped rungs is very different from the skyscraping poles with greased surfaces we currently suffer with.

Even beyond material resources, true equality requires a spreading of respect, status, and recognition to a broader range of social, productive, and cultural roles – what philosopher Elizabeth Anderson calls "democratic egalitarianism." People should be free to choose their own life trajectories, and our society needs to treat each outcome as a legitimate and dignified accomplishment, from trash collector to artist, from laborer to entrepreneur. While mostly requiring a massive and long-shot shift in our cultural values – reducing our fawning over celebrities, wealth, looks, and other elite indicators – it also depends on really reducing the disparities our society continues to create by its increasingly skewed salary differential for various roles.

Freedom

Liberty is a solitary status – an individual living on his own like the deserted island–seeking rebels in *Brave New World*; a nation standing by itself surrounded only by its own sovereignty. Freedom, in contrast, is only meaningful in the company of others, in society. Franklin Roosevelt's Four Freedoms – of speech and expression, to worship, from want and fear -- require cooperative work. Speech is only meaningful if there is someone listening; worship implies a congregation; other than existential fear of death or natural disaster, hunger, shelter, and care might potentially be satisfied by Robinson Crusoe–style personal effort but is usually a community project; fearful danger comes from other people. At the national level, freedom rests on the belief that sovereignty emanates from the aggregation of every individual citizen's inalienable human rights.

Freedom, at its best, is not merely liberty's lack of constraints -- freedom _from_ -- but also empowerment – the freedom _to_. Although it is a deeply social phenomenon, freedom has powerful implications for individuals. It is the cultural space and social support to become whoever and whatever you have the ability and wish to be, from your personal identity to productive enterprise. It is being – and feeling -- safe based on the appropriately enforced rule of democratically-created laws, in your home, on the streets, and in the legal use of your property. It is being in control of your own life choices and body, including women's freedom from sexual attack and to control their own reproductive functions. Freedom also implies the right of privacy, to be left alone – not to do what one wants regardless of its effect on others, but to withdraw for a while without losing the right to re-engage. Freedom for individuals in society, and for society as a whole, requires a level of material and personal security high enough to allow people to look beyond survival. It is living in a society organized to prevent anyone from falling through the cracks; to provide help when needed -- social welfare and economic systems with redistributive goals and active use of the state's market-shaping power.

At its worst, freedom is an excuse for self-aggrandizement at the expense of others or of nature, a reason to put oneself or one's group above the law, an ignoring of the fact that every individual or corporate achievement is only possible because of the collective presence and contributions of the surrounding society. This misuse of freedom, based on its reduction to unconstrained personal liberty regardless of the effect on others, also ends up as a short-sighted prioritizing of current benefits over stewardship for the future.

Democracy

Democracy is a political term, but it is relevant to nearly

every other aspect of our socio-economic lives. Politically, democracy is based on the principles of equal rights, open discussion, unhindered full participation at personally chosen levels of intensity, and uncoerced decision-making. Democracy also requires methods of limiting the power of the majority from running roughshod over the rights of minorities – an issue that the Constitution writers struggled with. We have also learned that a full realization of political democracy requires equality and the extension of democratic rights to other areas of social existence – reducing the gap between bottom and top and curtailing the ability of the rich to use their resources for coercion or manipulation.

Democracy is also vital because no society is perfectly homogeneous; every society has conflicting interests. Managing these tensions is an essential task of most political systems. Without a way of negotiating their differences, without participating in a mutually respectful and beneficial political process, groups become insecure and retreat into defensively looking out for only itself -- which then prompts similar behaviors by everyone else. Democracy, and the decision-making transparency its best examples embody, is what lets everyone accept the legitimacy of compromises. This is as true of economic decisions as of political ones.

Ronald Regan's slogan that "government is the problem" leaves us without any non-violent defense against the forces, groups, and people who would (intentionally or incidentally) harm or exploit us. It leaves us without any method for peacefully solving the problems that inevitably arise from the complexities of being human with others. Without methods of communal decision-making – without government – we are dropped into a jungle of all against all, a descent into the brutality of the stateless regions of the world whose massacres and disasters repeatedly show up in our headlines, a world in which violence rules. There is no anarchistic paradise of either the Ayn Rand egoist or the

Romantic "natural order" varieties waiting to emerge from that chaos – just insecurity and fear that cries out for authoritarian rescue. Government is more than a last-chance safety-net we turn to in absolute desperation. It is a positive, pro-active force for creating a world that makes humane life possible.

Equalitarian democracy helps build community. The political sphere is an important "public space" where we come together, where we experience the reality that our individual well-being is intimately tied to our common wealth.

Real politics, the everyday concerns of ordinary people with whom organizers need to work over the long haul in order to build the organizational strength to make good things happen, are about more than elections. They are also about the public programs and services that define the baseline of so many Americans' reality – from road construction to Social Security, from garbage collection to the police, from public health to education. The public sector is not just a safety net to protect us from smashing our faces when we suffer the inevitable stumble, nor merely a form of insurance through which we reduce the risk of personal disaster by aggregating small amounts of our collective resources, not only a key tool for creating the infrastructure and economic growth that funds our needs. Public programs are not a battleground, as conservatives claim, between dependency and independence. They are tools for community building. They are the foundation from which we build our lives and families, the resources and tools from which we create our society and our wealth. It is also the place that many of these ideals move from abstraction to reality.

In other words, the public sector – in its fullest meaning -- is both created by and the creator of our feelings of shared citizenship. It is what shapes our perceptions and attitudes about each other. If we believe that everyone is giving and getting back a fair share, if we know that our security and well-being depend on our continued collective willingness to treat each other's basic needs as legitimate as our own, if we understand that we rise or fall together – then we are laying the foundation for mutual acceptance and respect across all the otherwise difficult social barriers. We are also maintaining the conditions that allow democratic government to exist. No wonder that conservatives keep trying to kill Social Security and prevent Medicaid expansion!

Vision Is Political

Libertarians see the liberty of property owners to market their assets as the basis for all other rights, values, and well-being. Alt-right militants believe citizens' guns are the only guarantor of liberty from government control. Progressives describe freedom, equality, community, and democracy as interdependent rather than stand-alone values. It is the task of those working for positive social change to weave it all together in a vision that inspires hope, generates enthusiasm, and justifies long-term engagement.

Appeals for everyone to "be nice to each other" are morally valuable, but usually ineffectual on a larger scale, because all it takes are a few violators to kill the ceasefire and retrigger hostilities. This is as true domestically as it is internationally. Moral suasion is important, but there is simply no institution other than government with the mission and power to consistently protect citizens from the communal deterioration generated by the various types of competition that every society inherently develops. Evil is what happens when competition is allowed to freely run its unchecked course, when government does not do its mediating job, when organized citizenship fails. Politics is not external to our lives; it is part of what allows us to live humanely.

This can be a virtuous cycle. Acceptance of others is one of the bedrock cultural requirements for democracy; democracy is one of the drivers of good government; good government programs shape our daily lives and the cultural attitudes that emerge from them, including the acceptance of others. But history shows that without constant advocacy, this cycle is constantly broken.

Or perhaps, as current attacks on immigrants seem to suggest, too many of us have forgotten that all of our families were once strangers in this strange land. Perhaps we need to remember the Passover prayer to "let all who are hungry come to our table". We need to find ways to reinforce the visions that contribute to our sense of ourselves, collectively, as a community of "we, the people."

13. WHY THE PUBLIC SECTOR CAN'T BE RUN LIKE A BUSINESS:
Universal, Democratic, Open-ended

Those arguing for a business model for government must necessarily be ready to shut down all government functions that do not earn a profit, regardless of their contribution to our well-being. And, if the public sector is being run properly, that should mean every single one.

JOHN T. HARVEY, FORBES

It is to be regretted that the rich and powerful too often bend the acts of government to their own selfish purposes.

PRESIDENT ANDREW JACKSON

In a republic, as the Declaration of Independence states, governments derive "their just powers from the consent of the governed." In a democratic republic, citizens – acting through their government -- create an over-arching system of law and policy expressing how they wish to interact with each other and the conditions of life they wish to live within. Directly or indirectly, democratic governments are therefore ultimately responsible for the well-being and the protection of the rights of those living within its jurisdiction.

This doesn't mean that government is the total solution to societal difficulties – it is, in fact, often part of the problem. But, in most cases no solution is possible without it. Democratic government, for all its faults, is society's collective decision-making process and solution overseer. It is the space in which democracy plays out: In the midst of competing interests, finding a way to deal with problems or meet challenges that work for society as a whole requires government leadership to develop collective commitment, negotiate a plausible solution, and gather the needed resources.

Democratic governments provide methods of non-violent, legitimate, and enforceable decision-making – which is why one essential characteristic of sovereign governments is having a monopoly on the legitimate use of physical force for domestic order and national security, a role which can be delegated but never removed. Without effective democratic government we are dropped into a jungle of all against all. It is, at best, a society in which the ruthless and powerful can impose their will on everyone else; in which the weak have no place to turn. There is no anarchistic paradise of either the Ayn Rand egoist or the Romantic "natural order" varieties waiting to emerge from that chaos – just insecurity and fear that cries out for authoritarian rescue and humanitarian aid.

Since the Enlightenment, government has become synonymous with state power and nations, and those with citizenship. It's a circular relationship. As Jill Lapore explains in *This America: The Case for the Nation,* human rights are innate but unenforceable outside national governments. The whole construct "rested on the idea that the equal rights of citizens can only be guaranteed by their becoming the citizens of nations.... No nations, no constitutions; no constitutions, no citizens; no citizens, no rights" with which to demand that government serves their collective will.

In the early twentieth century, Calvin Coolidge said that "the business of government is business." In recent decades, there has been increasing demands that government not merely promote business but be run like a business – or simply cut down to minute size so deregulated private enterprise can take over its functions from prisons to social services, from policing to urban planning. The argument is that government is slow, inefficient, indecisive, wasteful, inconsistent and absorbs resources that could be better used elsewhere.

(Because of the visibility of public sector problems and inadequacies, we tend to ignore the fact that private sector organizations and leaders are just as likely to be perpetuators of "waste, fraud, and abuse" with even larger and more destructive societal impact than government. But it's all hidden behind the screen of "business confidentiality," "property rights," and the mythology of "consumer choice." In business, nothing is wrong so long as the bottom line is positive. It's a taken-for-granted double standard that unfairly makes the public sector look bad.)

However, from a progressive perspective, exactly the opposite is true. Not only can government not be run like a business, not only should for-profit operations be allowed to replace public functions, but it would be good for society – and democracy – if many public sector values and principles were incorporated into business operations.

Politics Is Supposed To Be Messy

This is not to say that complaints about government in-efficiency, ineffectiveness, and bureaucracy aren't valid. In the USA, the public sector's incredibly slow and dispersed decision-making processes were originally built into our federal and state constitutions primarily to defend elites from the "excesses" of democracy. But it also plays a role in protecting citizens' rights – as Trump's inability to force key state Republicans to distort election results demonstrated.

At its best, a society's political system allows competing inter-ests, ideologies, and visions to find a way to live together with-out violence, perhaps to even work together. It is the infamous sausage-making of compromise and incremental adjustments. At the same time, as an instrument of the existing society – and therefore its established hierarchies – the political system is also supposed to prevent radical change. This requires that "extreme" proposals get watered down (or repressed) and negotiated into a workable moderation. The terms of the negotiation are not "right and wrong" but "interests" and "messaging." This makes normal politics seem infuriatingly superficial, irrelevant, mor-ally bankrupt, and dangerous to those engaged in a moral cru-sade, or who believe that their dignity or survival is at stake, or who know that radical change is needed for justice or prosperity or simply survival.

The failure of government to deal with major problems – even to efficiently perform ordinary functions from trash pick-up to snow removal -- undermines public confidence in the value of public action – which is one of the reasons that anti-government conservatives are so willing to let public program operations deteriorate. The widespread chaos around the initial distribution of the Covid-19 vaccines – rooted, partly, in the Trump Administration's refusal to provide national guidance – fed into the widespread anxiety about the pandemic and prompted governors to turn to private businesses rather than work through the public health system.

All this makes advocacy hard. Advocacy depends on some amount of hope, which is hard to maintain when the government whose action is needed moves so slowly, acts in such awkward and inefficient ways, and has so much difficulty carrying a vision through to long-term conclusion. It's important to acknowledge all the things that make public sector-led positive change difficult. And then it's even more important to discuss why it's worth the effort.

Universal Service Imperative

If customers are not able to pay enough, they are no longer served. But public schools are expected to educate everyone, no matter their family income – or even their interest in and aptitude for learning. The motor vehicle department has to serve all citizens, no matter how difficult their problems or personalities. Our laws require that people in wheelchairs are able to cross the street, without charging them extra for the curb cuts and beeping walk signals. The universal service imperative of public sector programs is a vital contribution to legitimizing the demands of minority groups for equal access to quality public services.

The universality of public services is also important because it gives the entire society a stake in their existence, continued funding, and quality. Programs only for poor people inevitably end up being poor programs. Public housing was allowed to collapse once it became the residence of last resort for the poor and non-white. In contrast, Social Security, used by nearly everyone, is still considered one of the untouchable "third rails" of politics – and its existence as an essential connection between everyone and the government is a key reason that right-wing ideologists repeatedly try to kill it through privatization.

In recent years, ascendant conservative forces have driven responsibility for dealing with many problems to ever-lower levels of government. Their argument is that the more local a decision, the more it expresses popular desire. However, the lower the level of government the less its financial resources and staff expertise. By the time responsibility reaches the local level, the reality is that absent an active and permanent effort to mobilize less well-off citizens, local governments tend to be under the sway of local elites – mostly the larger businesses as well as the real estate and construction industries who traditionally want to keep taxes low and regulation light so resist expanding the scope of government programs. As a result, the conservative push for devolution of responsibility tends to push problems down until they fall below the jurisdictional level at which the situation can be effectively managed or needed resources raised, thereby making it unsolvable and "proving" that government doesn't work. The resulting inadequacies give credence to Ronald Reagan's mantra that "government is the problem."

All of which leaves families dependent on their private resources, which means that those without simply do without, and find it increasingly hard to do anything about it. An eroding faith in government also undermines people's willingness to be active citizens, making it easier for anti-democrats to institute restrictions in their opponents' voting rights.

Furthermore, while the problems government agencies are asked to solve are often complex, with connections to a range of factors from international to local, and extending across many aspects of people's lives, any particular agency's scope of authority is often dysfunctionally narrow. Lack of inter-departmental coordination is endemic to almost all large organizations, including private corporations. But it is visible in the public sector. Transportation agencies, for example, have no direct power over – and often little coordination with – land use, although the two are intrinsically linked.

Open-Ended Scope Of Responsibility

A business has a legally clear and simple goal: making money. A business gets to define the limits of its products and services — to say that its products will serve some purposes and not others, that its services will do certain things but not others – beyond which it is not responsible. Progressives have repeatedly tried to expand the list of private sector goals through the creation of "B-corps" and the promotion of a "triple bottom line." There have been efforts to get corporations to pay more attention to workforce development, environmental stewardship, public service, and community benefits. But, except as required by law, these have only endured to the extent they are tied to the core directive of profit. Investors want a return. Firms that keep increasing profits survive; those that don't disappear.

The public sector is not allowed to do triage, to cull the best and leave the rest. Government is ultimately responsible for the entire society's well-being. Not only does the public sector have a constantly evolving and endlessly contentious mission, there is no simple or agreed upon way to measure its success in achieving that mission – whatever it is. Schools, for example, are ultimately responsible for creating the next generation of adults in all their roles as citizens, parents, friends, workers, and individuals – with endless debates about what those roles look like and how to train children for them. (Of course, putting this entire responsibility on one institution is a prescription for failure.) This leads to the robust and never-ending political debates that are the essence of democracy, but that also make it difficult for public sector departments to focus their efforts and measure their progress – and for the public to evaluate their level of success.

Still, the open-ended nature of public responsibility is an essential foundation for demanding that government meet people's needs as the people experience those needs rather than as "experts" and "professionals" interpret the situation.

OPERATIONAL COMPLEXITY

Public programs have – or should have – ill-defined boundaries. Of course, this contradicts the first rule of management: stay focused, keep it simple, avoid mission creep. However, every policy and program has externalities, "side issues" – effects on the job market, the environment, the surrounding neighborhoods – that are capable of multiplying the social value or turning into unintended, damaging consequences. It is incumbent on public sector leaders to start from the widest possible perspective, to go out of their way to maximize the positive externalities beyond their official scope and budget. But all this makes public sector leadership much more complicated, important, and (given the ability of the private sector to pay high salaries) undercompensated given the needed level of skill. And, unfortunately, really great managers are very rare – in the private as much as the public sectors.

If a factory doesn't produce profits (and sometimes even if it does), it gets closed or moved. If a firm's product doesn't do well, it gets discontinued. If a business employee is failing to perform, he gets fired. Public sector employment has much more complicated dynamics. In addition to finding someone capable of performing job-description tasks, government hiring is often used to redress disparities in the business labor market and to serve as a slightly better model of how to operationalize evolving social policies. As an expression of the political process, public programs are – and should be – responsive to the needs of the larger population. The mass immigration of Irish and German refugees in the 1800s swelled the cities. Local governments began massive infrastructure projects (stepping on the toes of private firms providing similar services). These projects not only served the needs of the growing population but provided work for the immigrant laborers.

Yes, having to satisfy complex and broad public needs probably reduces the task-efficiency of government offices. Still, given the huge scope of public sector responsibility, it is on the whole a good thing that government agencies see themselves as pursuing multiple goals.

RISK-TAKING COMPLEXITY

Our scandal-hungry media and politicians' re-election worries tend to make mistakes more politically damaging than successes are beneficial. Our political system punishes exposed failures more than it rewards incremental advances. Politicians, and those who work under them, tend to be risk averse, with a short-term focus usually extending no further than the next likely change of administration. All this fosters organizational cultures that teach public employees that the best career move is to keep your head down, to do only what you've been told to do. Advocates – and politicians – need to put some energy into helping the public understand that occasional failures are the price of the innovation and flexibility that lead to effective operations.

Public Input, Transparency, Accountability

Except to the extent they need government permits or investments and loans, private firms don't need to listen to anyone's advice or let anyone know what they are doing.

In the public sector, open records laws and public input processes are mandated -- even when ignored or weak, transparency and stakeholder participation are principles that validate advocates' demands. Secrecy not only allows corruption; it also prompts poorer quality plans and inadequate evaluations. Even more dangerously, it undermines public trust in democracy.

For years, "ordinary" people were excluded from public programs' decision-making processes. Then, as one result of
the Civil Rights Movement, starting in 1964 with the Great
Society's anti-poverty legislation promising "maximum feasible
participation of the poor", public input became an increasingly
important component of many areas of policy making, particularly around housing and community development issues. The
massive, nation-wide push-back against continued city-destroy-
ing highway construction made public input processes a central
part of transportation planning as well– the iconic examples of
which were the successful fights to stop the Cross Manhattan
highway and the Boston Inner Belt.

There hasn't been a complete change. Official "participation"
and "input" methods often leave citizens feeling that they are
being patronized or ignored – getting only minor or symbolic
gestures in response to their demands. The core aspects of what
the bureaucrats want remain unchanged – usually promoting
business growth and profit over neighborhood stability or low-
income services. The feeling in many communities is that sitting at the table isn't enough; they want decision-making authority. The slogan is "power, not participation."

Complicating this democratizing demand is that the number
and variety of stakeholders for public projects varies according
to the size and impact of the proposed program or work. Boston
would not be the city it is, and most of eastern Massachusetts
would have long-since stagnated, if a dozen towns in the middle
of the state had not been taken over by the state and buried
under the Quabbin Reservoir. The history and community life
of those towns was lost but the state laid a needed foundation
for the future. Similarly, given current rules for citizen input, it's
not clear that New York's Central Park, Chicago's El network, or
San Francisco's bridges – all essential to current life and prosperity -- would be possible to build today.

And sometimes a hyper-local perspective is destructive in another way. As the repeated failure of efforts to build affordable housing shows, the more local and narrow the boundaries of the discussion the more likely it is that "abutters" fall into NIMBY self-interest, which can also be expressive of their own prejudices, rejecting anything that changes their own situation or allows "less desirable" poorer people to join them.

At a minimum, those most immediately affected, particularly negatively, by a program or project must have their voices heard and their losses compensated. Even if those local interests are outweighed by larger needs, their input can lead to better plans. In fact, most proposals are improved after public discussion, including advocates' inputs. Like finding ways to preserve minority rights in a majoritarian political system, this is a tension that is worth having.

Finally, government is accountable, either directly through elections or indirectly through lawsuits. The only direct check on corporate behavior comes from majority shareholders – minority owners have little power and the public has none other than a massive consumer boycott, something that is extremely difficult to organize and sometimes either legally challengeable or practically impossible. Of course, the accountability of government depends on equal access to the voting system, with government using every possible method to maximize participation – something Republicans are increasingly opposing. But no matter how violated in practice, public accountability is an inherent principle of democracy.

Ownership And Funding

Private firms are owned by investors who, legally, have final say over all decisions. Decision-making is an insider's prerogative. No outsider expects to be able to tell Coca-Cola what to do; we can subsidize, regulate, protest, or boycott – all from the outside. But we can't decide. And investors are not doing charity. They invest money in expectation of getting a profitable return later on. A firm's expected ability to provide that return determines how easy it will be to secure credit, get loans, and sell stock.

The Adam Smith vision is that competitive private markets are the democratizing alternative to monarchal monopolies and irresponsible absolutism; that the pursuit of private gain by a multitude of actors, each driven to improve products and service under the pressure of peers with relatively similar market power, will collectively lead to public good.

Today, however, our competitive marketplace is hardly that. Despite the huge numbers and visibility of small and medium-sized business, almost every major US industry is dominated by three or fewer corporations. Their owners and managers have an inherent incentive and the market-dominating ability to externalize costs to their workforce, neighborhood, environment, nation, and world – pollution, climate change, safety and health, family and community stress, social stability, even national security. The entrance of a disruptive new technology or business model, or a new player from a space previously outside the traditional economic boundaries, may occasionally upset the apple cart. But after a period of crisis – which often causes thousands of workers to lose their jobs, their families often ending up suffering serious financial and health hardships – the situation restabilizes into a new oligopoly.

It is not that the owners and managers are evil people, although some really don't care about anything but themselves. It's that market dynamics inherently push them, to the extent not prohibited by law or other external constraints, to do whatever they can to increase profits. Ironically, the pursuit of ever-more risky increases in profit over the course of every business cycle, and the upward redistribution of wealth and power intrinsic in inadequately regulated markets, leads to boom-and-bust cycles that destabilize capitalist economies and societies.

PUBLIC GOODS

In contrast, the public sector is "owned" by everyone. There are no outsiders. We believe that public workers work for us, that public organizations exist for our benefit. This is based in everyone's right to vote. But it extends into our attitudes about other things: everyone has an opinion about the way our schools should be run and feels free to demand that school authorities listen. The democratic foundation of the public sector gives everyone a stake and a voice.

This can make long-term planning and even immediate operational decisions exceedingly difficult. Bosses change every few years, priorities change even more often, and avoiding scandal is sometimes more important than improving performance. Long-term commitments get ignored after each change of administration.

But for all its problems, the existence of a public sector is the necessary basis for the existence of public goods – the collectively-shared resources that enable people to live with enough safety and well-being to see each other as members of the same community rather than as fight-to-survive rivals, preferably provided in ways that promote collaboration and mutual aid through public programs that inspire faith in government's ability to serve its people and perform its tasks. This is the guarantee of democracy we need.

PAYING THE PIPER

It is also important that public sector organizations are, at least partly, funded through taxes. Taxes are a collective investment in the continued health of our overall society, without which none of our personal lives and business activities would be possible. It's true that taxpayers have little choice about paying, no matter how dire their own financial situation, or how poorly public services are delivered, or even whether or not they are direct users or beneficiaries of a particular service. Still, as Winston Churchill said, "taxes are the price we pay for civilization." It is an indicator of how far American culture has been pushed to the right that this now sounds like a radical idea.

The mutual aid and insurance aspects of taxation – through which (in a progressive system) everyone contributes into a common pot according to their income and wealth with the knowledge that resources will be made available to them when needed – is a vital foundation for the cultural awareness that we are all interdependent, with overlapping lives and intertwined destinies. Taxes – if self-imposed through a democratic process, efficiently collected, and effectively used – are part of democracy. Taxes are, by definition, political. Public debate about the level and use of tax money is a vital motivation for citizenship.

MIXED ECONOMIES

Almost no one, at least in the United States, still promotes the original socialist vision that all economic activity would be run by a centralized government. Progressives now promote a spectrum of options from public agencies (like the TVA), to B-corporations and other "multiple mission" businesses, to non-profits, to worker-cooperatives (perhaps modeled on the Basque-region's Mondragon system), to small and perhaps even large for-profit enterprises. The issue is not the form of the enterprise, but how well it fits into a democratically shaped overall market, and its effect on the common good.

As Elizabeth Warren said in one campaign interview,
> There is nobody in this country who got rich on his own – nobody.... You built a factory out there? Good for you. You moved your goods to market on the roads the rest of us paid for. You hired workers the rest of us paid to educate. You were safe in your factory because of police-forces and fire-forces that the rest of us paid for. You didn't have to worry that marauding bands would come and seize everything at your factory...because of the work the rest of us did...God bless – keep a big hunk of it. But part of the underlying social contract is that you take a hunk of that and pay forward for the next kid who comes along.

Democracy

In principle, even if not always in fact, governments are required to serve everyone; business only serves customers from whom a profit can be gained. Governments are ultimately responsible for the smooth functioning and well-being of every part of society; business only undertakes tasks from which a profit can be gained. Government hiring and labor relations have to contribute to the realization of a broad range of social, cultural, political, and legal goals; beyond legal compliance, business's operational decisions are entirely focused on increasing profit with the attendant imperative to externalize costs. Public sector organizations are supposed to be transparent and their efforts are evaluated across a broad range of criteria; corporations are allowed to hide most information about themselves from public disclosure and their level of success is solely measured by the increase in profits and ownership value (e.g., share prices), often over the short term. Governments are democratically "owned" by the entire citizenry from whom public revenues are raised, primarily through taxes which serve as a pooled insurance and investment fund; business is owned by those who have invested capital, and exists to provide a return on that investment.

Business leaders use their wealth and economic influence to shape the political system to protect and profit themselves. That's their job. Government is supposed to serve us all. Government can't be run like a business because it has a different mission, purpose, and underlying values than business. Government's job is not to make profits for a small group of owners but, rather, to make possible the best possible lives for the entire population. As the Constitution says, it's "We, the People."

The public sector can certainly benefit from the adoption of many business practices, from a focus on customer service to more efficient work flow, from measurement of operations and outcomes to external accountability. But no matter how needed these practices may be, no matter how much the public sector can benefit from their use, there is a fundamental difference between the two sectors that will perpetually lead to differences. The public sector rests on a foundation of universalizing democracy, mutually supportive community, collectively generated prosperity and well-being. Business is ultimately based on the assumption that public good primarily emerges from the pursuit of private profit on behalf of self-serving owners – as Gordon Gekko famously put it in the movie *Wall Street*, "greed is good!"

Demanding that government "be a business" -- or "get out of the way" so business can do public work better -- is destructive of both democracy and the public good. There are a variety of ways that governments cannot –and should not – be like business. And it is exactly in upholding and demanding these differences that advocates protect democracy as well as push forward on their particular issue. Advocates are not only change agents around their particular issue. By working to make government better serve the people, they are also democrats – preservers of both individual rights and social well-being.

14. PUBLIC-PRIVATE PARTNERSHIPS:

Creating Public Value through Privatizing, Contracting, and Collaboration

Alliances and partnerships produce stability when they reflect realities and interests.
STEPHEN KINZER & TAE YOO

If someone promises to do great things, ask them first for something small, like a bridge or a cow.
LEONEL GÓMEZ VIDES, IN WHAT YOU HAVE HEARD IS TRUE, BY
CAROLYN FORCHÉ

Public-Private Partnerships (P3) are increasingly being offered as the solution to social problems that advocates are protesting. P3 arrangements are between a public agency and a for-profit or non-profit entity. There is potentially much to be gained by harnessing the speedy decision-making, operational flexibility, innovativeness, access to capital, and potential efficiency of non-government actors. Tae Yoo, Senior Vice President at Cisco Corporation, points out that "when private sector, government, social, and philanthropic leaders apply innovative partnerships and technologies to address social challenges and build sustainable communities, the impact is multiplied." In a time of tight budgets and escalating demands, it would be unwise to pass up such opportunities.

However, P3s are often deceptively used as a way for governments to cut budgets, or for conservative politicians to downsize government while claiming that supposed increased efficiencies won't turn reduced expenditures into reduced services. Agency officials sometimes use P3s as a way to shift blame for inadequate public investment or poor management on to outside vendors. Even if everything is honestly presented and properly run, P3s accomplishments don't always match the promise. If not carefully designed, creatively led, properly managed, effect-ively run, and repeatedly evaluated and improved, partnerships will fail – or at least not live up to initial expectations. It is in-accurate and confusing to lump all P3 activity into one category.

Business consultants use a "division of risk and reward" frame-work to divide P3s into categories correlating the degree of uncertainty about gaining the anticipated reward with the amount of that reward. It is a useful analysis, but it misses the point. There is nothing wrong with public enterprises earning and returning excess revenue for additional public investment. But that is usually simply a side-benefit of a P3. The primary purpose of a P3 is increased public value which takes many forms beyond money, much less the division of potential profit. Strengthening the social safety net and family stability; increas-ing acess to good jobs; enhancing people's faith in democratic government; reducing disparities -- all these are public values whose reduction to dollars misses the main point.

The three types of P3s discussed here – privatization, contract-ing-out, and collaborations – each have different underlying as-sumptions, resulting in different roles for the public and non-public partners, and therefore providing different types and amounts of value for the public footing the bill. The nature of the P3 also depends on the type of organization on each side of the relationship. Is the public side represented by a government agency or a quasi-public organization? Is the private side a for-profit business, "social impact" investor, a rich individual, a non-profit foundation, social service agency, or foundation, some-time even a community corporation or citizens' group?

Understanding these differences is vital for deciding which are actually good deals – delivering meaningful public value at an acceptable cost.

The Public Partner
Governments and their agencies are unique in their re-

quired universality, accountability, and democratic oversight. Government is constitutionally required to serve everyone without discrimination. It is legally required to explain what it is doing, where the money is coming from, and what the funding is being used for. It is subject to the policies and laws established through our (theoretically) democratic political processes. The public value of government programs, services, and facilities is not merely "the thing itself" but the surrounding side effects and externalities: the degree to which it contributes to the entire population's ability to participate in the larger society. In other words, the degree to which it counteracts the tendency of our economic and political systems to create inequality of access, wealth, and opportunity.

It is possible to design the contract, Memorandum of Understanding (MOU), or other document that defines the relationship between the government and its partner in ways that carry forward the values and benefits that government provides, and that includes on-going methods of evaluation and enforcement for living up to those obligations. But it takes political leaders absolutely committed to maximizing public value rather than saving money, negotiators with very specific expertise, program managers and technical experts with the ability and backing needed to stay on top of the partnership through its entire life-cycle, and long-term public support. Doable, but hard. Typically, giving over a government program, service, or facility to an outside entity weakens the expectation – and likelihood – that larger public values will be sought or realized.

It is even harder if the public partner is a quasi-public (aka quasi-governmental) organization – an independent agency separate from the Executive with self-financing authority (i.e., issuing bonds or charging user fees) run by appointed boards. Massachusetts, for example, has 42 quasi-publics ranging in size from six to over 6,000 employees responsible for a variety of purposes -- from rail and transit systems (MBTA), to water provision and discharge (MWRA), to harbor management (Port Authority) to managing public pensions (PERAC), to economic development (MassDevelopment), to health insurance (the Connector), to cultural support (Cultural Council), and more.

Quasi-public organizations tend to do a good job at their assigned tasks. But the degree of public accountability varies. Depending on state and federal law, quasi-publics may or may not be subject to open meeting or other public records requirements, may or may not be required to issue periodic financial and performance reports for review by a designated public agency, and may or may not be subject to periodic re-authorization. Massachusetts does a better job of setting up quasi-publics than most states. Even so, until sued by the ACLU in 2014, many of these agencies, ironically including the Northeastern Massachusetts Law Enforcement Council (NEMLEC), refused to even honor public requests for information. In New York, Robert Moses used his unsupervised control of the region's Triborough Bridge and Tunnel Authority to ram destructive highways and urban renewal through neighborhoods across the city.

Privatization

Privatization involves selling off, giving away, or granting a very long-term lease for the use of public assets, usually to a for-profit corporation but occasionally to a non-profit or community corporation. At its best, privatization hopes to make up for a previous long-term and anticipated future lack of public resources (money and managerial skill) by utilizing non-government administrative/operational expertise and for-profits' ability to tap into a broader range of investor and banking capital. In addition to the one-time ownership-transfer fee and occasional revenue-sharing agreements, the private partner often promises an initial investment for upgrading or expansion. Political leaders typically promise that this will lead to better services and that they will use the new revenue to focus attention on improving the remaining publicly financed services.

To make it work, the new owner is allowed to treat the asset or program as their private property – charging user fees, deciding on how to run things and who to hire and serve, and retaining any profits. In some cases, the give-away is the opposite of revenue sharing -- a promise of continued public subsidies to guarantee future profits, either directly to the acquiring firm or indirectly through infrastructure improvements or other public expenditures. In addition, the new owner is released from any social obligation not explicitly included in the sale agreement or applicable to all businesses. In theory, being the owner gives companies a vested interest in regular maintenance and continued investments to ensure the long-term viability of the privatized property.

Politically, privatization is usually a tactic for dealing with embarrassing failures or declining public revenue, or for reducing future growth in public budgets, or simply based on the belief that government should not be involved in that activity. Not surprisingly, privatization is at the heart of most current Republican proposals for infrastructure development – highways, airports, canals, even the International Space Station. Currently "free" (meaning tax-financed) infrastructure – roads, bridges, parks – will become tolled. People who cannot pay will not be able to use the facility, or will have to reduce their spending on other things. The majority of our nation's infrastructure that does not have sufficient profit-generating potential will be allowed to continue deteriorating. The effect, occurring predominately in rural areas and urban low-income or non-white neighborhoods, will have the predictable negative effects on the underserved populations' standard of living. It is the normal kind of income-based rationing that usually goes unnoticed in our market-based economy.

Implicitly, if not explicitly, privatization rests on a belief that private, market-based activity is a better creator of public value than public programs. Or even more bluntly, that government simply cannot run anything well. However, unless carefully written into the transfer agreement, the loss of public control and oversight inherent in privatization eliminates requirements for universal service, equitable access and hiring, environmental protection, or any social goal other than that required by the general market regulations for all businesses – which are themselves generally under attack by the same groups pushing for privatization.

MARKET IMPERATIVES

In practice, the imperative of for-profit firms to steadily increase their returns usually has more impact on their long-term management of the asset than their supposed ability to run things efficiently. Privatization regularly leads to service reductions or price increases that particularly hit those most in need. Over time, products/services are reshaped and repriced to serve those whose patronage provides the most profit, leaving behind everyone else – usually the less affluent and less white. Whenever possible, costs are "externalized," shifting the often environmental or public health burden to taxpayers or future generations. Services that do not contribute to the bottom line will be cut. Public input into decision-making will be reduced or eliminated.

Selling public assets is complicated. It is often hard to determine the appropriate sale price. The numbers may sound large, but they are often less than the full public value – which includes not only public access but also the ability to hold government accountable for its equity and universal service commitments in the programming, upkeep, and decision-making processes. Furthermore, asset sales are often done when the public sector is under economic duress, making it harder to prevent sweetheart deals. When this happens on a large scale the opportunities for insider trading are multiplied – the "shock treatment" that Russia and Chile applied to "de-socialize" their economies turned massive amounts of public property over to the oligarchs who now support Putin's authoritarian government and stand in the way of Chile's efforts to democratize its military-imposed constitution.

Ironically, the higher user fees required for profitable operation of privatized assets and programs will probably reduce their use – which, in some cases, will reduce environmentally damaging activity that burdens us all. However, in the absence of off-setting rebates of some kind, this will hit some families, particularly low-income families, the hardest. For example, privatized highways will induce people to drive less, reducing congestion and gas-engine pollution, but adversely affecting those with no option but to drive. And, should the trains and transit also be privatized, leading to price increases or service reductions, there will be even less incentive to use them instead.

STILL, SOMETIMES...

Public-value enhancing privatization is possible. It is possible that the money paid for a privatized asset would not be simply used as a one-time fix for a budget shortfall or to allow tax cuts that further reduce public resources. And sale or ownership transfer of public assets can be appropriate in some situations. A property may have no current or anticipated future use – although the future is hard to predict. The price offered for the purchase of an asset – based on its perceived value for some profit-making venture -- may be so high that it totally dwarfs any current or possible public use value.

A fool-proof sales agreement might lead to real service improvements while retaining significant levels of service to the previously underserved, public transparency, and local decision-making. Private firms, bound by the impact-focused continuing oversight written into purchase or lease agreements, might successfully increase operational efficiencies, expand the user base, improve the marketing, and reduce the per-user costs without lowering working conditions – while being contractually required to the asset's future development into the city's overall goals and master plans.

The transfer of ownership might be contractually guaranteed to

lead to a full range of irresistibly positive – and carefully measured – complementary outcomes, from significant job and tax
revenue growth to environmental and social well-being, from
local-hiring and training program guarantees to meaningful
revenue-growth sharing, with penalties for non-compliance. It
may be possible to surround the sale with so many requirements
and such powerful incentives for overachievement that it will
provide a quantitative and qualitative abundance of public value
across the full range of public sector concerns – although the
profits from such a contract are likely to be low and therefore the
interest of profit-seeking firms minimal.

DOUBLE REVERSE

In the absence of all these circumstances, the most damaging
effect of the push for privatization is that it makes it politically
harder to do the reverse -- bringing productive components of
the economy under more effective public direction. A lot could
be gained by requiring every corporation over a certain size to
include local, state, and federal government appointees (as well
as labor representatives!) on its board. There are some businesses whose public value would be enormously increased by
being publicly owned, preferably by a properly designed quasi-
public. The Tennessee Valley Authority is a powerful example of
what can be done – as well as what can go wrong if quasi-publics
are left unsupervised.

What if instead of bailing out the collapsing banks and General
Motors in 2009, Obama had threatened to nationalize them or
demanded the restructuring of their Board? What if any use
of taxpayer-funded research would require not only appropriate
fees and a share of the profits but also a voice in what is done (or
at a minimum, what is not done) with the information? What
if key portions of the fossil fuel industry, or just of regional gas
utilities, were bought out by public agencies and the resulting
firms charged with a rapid move to more sustainable energy production? The public would get fewer dollars but enormous value
from their investment.

Contracting Out

Contracting, or outsourcing, is enormously varied and is by far the most common form of public-private partnership. Fundamentally, it describes hiring a non-government group – again, anything on a spectrum from a community corporation to a non-profit to private business – to carry out particular tasks, run particular programs, or manage particular public resources. While it is assumed that the vendor will be serving its own interests/mission as much as the sponsor's (for example, a for-profit vender intends to make money from the arrangement), "contracting out" retains – at least theoretically – a high degree of public oversight, responsibility, and accountability. While letting go of operations, the government agency potentially retains control of planning in response to both the political system's demands and the region's future needs. Even when planning is also outsourced, the public agency is still supposedly overseeing the contractor, primarily by setting appropriate goals and ongoing performance evaluation criteria in the contract.

In the private sector, contracting out is touted as a way to focus managerial attention on a smaller workforce and core competencies. Pushing secondary tasks to outside firms increases the flexibility to change vendors as the need for secondary tasks changes – and, to the extent that the vendor market is composed of small, competitive firms, to repeatedly lower both labor and overhead costs. These aspects of outsourcing are not as relevant – or desirable – in a government context since public programs have a broader range of goals than operational efficiency and low cost. But the business world's enthusiasm for outsources does add to the generally positive view of these proposals in the mainstream corporate media.

Usually, contracting out involves ongoing payments from the public agency to the contractor. Sometimes, although not often, the contractor is also allowed to keep all or some of any user fees that its activity generates; in some cases, this may even substitute for agency payments. While some vendors' bids may include bringing assets and resources to the partnership, and while they may buy and retain ownership of certain equipment needed for the work, they do not have an equity/ownership interest in the core program or property. The gain in public value comes, in theory, from "lifting the bureaucratic wet blanket" off managers, workers, and operations. At its best, contracted vendors are able to significantly improve the efficiency of a program through the application of better operational systems and labor relations, new technologies, decision-making flexibility, and speed.

However, in contrast to nearly all arguments given to sell an outsourcing proposal, research on outsourcing reveals that, when well done in ways that maximize the overall public value, contracting out is seldom less costly overall than direct public agency operations. Proponents seldom reveal that good oversight requires the continuing development of in-house technical expertise in the public agency as well as extensive training in the new skill of "management through contracts." Neither is it acknowledged that larger-than anticipated numbers of public sector professional staff are invariably still needed for setting the planning agenda as well as operational oversight and contractual renegotiations.

In fact, a vendor may even be more expensive than in-house operations, depending on how risks are apportioned. For example, a vendor that has to supply fuel for a transit system will have to pad their bid in order to cover uncertainty about future price increases while the public agency firm would merely pay the actual cost when due.

A GROWTH STRATEGY
Still, if the goal is to improve and increase public service, and if the government is willing to maintain or perhaps even increase a program's funding, outsourcing can be a powerful tool. Private firms can draw on wider pools of expertise (and pay higher

salaries) than most agencies or governments. They can make operational decisions and implement changes faster with fewer required stakeholder negotiations. Having experience in a variety of settings under a variety of contracted terms, the vendor may be more creative and open to innovation than agency staff. In the best imaginable circumstances, future cost increases can be reduced by encouraging vendors to explore post-selection opportunities for innovation, operational changes, and other efficiency-increasing tactics -- although, despite the potential benefits, giving up service-model control would be hard for most public agencies to accept.)

Outsourcing may make sense even in more troubled situations. If the public program is significantly dysfunctional and the agency in charge is simply incapable of regaining control, then at least temporary outsourcing may be the only way out of the box. Similarly, if the agency/program needs significant new investment to get back on its feet, but there is an action-killing public perception based on past experience that the agency is incompetent and bloated, then even a well-meaning and highly skilled leadership team might find outsourcing a necessary step towards regaining public support. However, in either case, the odds of success diminish if the emphasis is on cost reductions rather than improved operations.

OR THE OPPOSITE

In reality, outsourcing, like privatization, is most often used as part of a budget-cutting or tax cut campaign, which undermines the vendor's ability to deliver promised benefits. When the primary focus is cutting costs and reducing public expenditures, the vendor's hoped-for efficiency is seldom enough to pay for improved service past an initial burst, much less more indirect public value. Under revenue pressures, vendors almost always end up having to implement some combination of lower wages, worsening working conditions, reduced service and maintenance, increased usage fees, or failure to invest in future technologies or upgrades.

The commercialization of public assets and services can also change people's perception and relationship to the program. A recent visitor to Yosemite National Park reported not being able to find the Visitor Center, which turned out to be tucked into a private concession and staffed by sales people. The message, she felt, was that this iconic public place no longer was a fully public venue – no longer "hers" or "ours."

Even if contracting is done with non-profits, problems may emerge. In New York City, about 20 private non-profit Conservancies raise money and have some degree of operational authority over particular parks. The most famous, and richest, is the Central Park Conservancy, which has been key to the phenomenal rejuvenation of that once-neglected and unsafe area. However, lacking Central Park's wealthy neighbors, dozens of smaller parks in less prominent locations continue to deteriorate. A proposal to require that the rich conservancies share a small percentage of their funds with less-endowed areas was defeated because of the fear that it would discourage donations from wealthy neighbors. Instead, the city administration stepped up with $285 million in public money for the low-status areas and merely got the rich conservancies to agree to provide limited technical assistance and some in-kind resources to the less endowed. This allowed the rich to pay for at least some of the high level of maintenance they expect in the public facilities they use. It also undercuts any argument that outsourcing does much to reverse market-power rationing.

ADVICE FROM THE FIELD

A gathering of transit-system outsourcing public and private sector practitioners at MIT listed some of the essentials of successful contracting. First was the requirement of acknowledging and implementing the continued public responsibility to set direction and evaluation metrics along with ongoing and checkpoint operational and contract oversight. Contractually requiring shared data collection and storage systems is key to this.

Second was the need to be extremely smart about how to align the vendor's profit-seeking motivation with the agency's public mission at both the macro and micro levels. Non-performance penalties are popular, but can only be applied across a relatively small number of metrics and simply create a floor rather than raise the ceiling. Positive incentives for securing better-than-mandated outcomes along an extremely broad range of criteria, focused as much on the customer experience as on operational details, are much more likely to focus the vendor's attention and stimulate its creativity.

Third was avoiding confusion and potential buck-passing by establishing clear delineation of roles, responsibilities, and areas of leadership for each contractual party. For example, the agency can focus on planning while the vendor focuses on making operations more efficient. Related to this was the suggestion that agencies not lock-in a specific service model at the RFP stage – meaning that request for proposal (RFP) responses and signed contracts are treated as the starting point for continuing improvements rather than a fixed description of operational promises.

These practitioners suggested allowing the RFP-winning vendor to propose service-improving or cost-reducing efficiencies beyond what their bid originally described. Attendees pointed out that few vendors would be likely to suggest new, breakthrough ideas before the RFP was awarded because nothing would prevent their competitors from simply using the idea in their own bid. Several people pointed out that a vendor stuck with a fixed operational model can only create efficiencies through cost-cutting and job intensification, both of which are likely to reduce rather than improve customer service and satisfaction. However, it was also acknowledged that allowing post-selection changes to the contract would require extremely careful RFP wording and very brave political leadership.

An explicit theme of the discussion was that firing current

workers to make room for vendor staff, reducing current employees' pay, or worsening their working conditions, was a prescription for failure. One repeatedly successful contractor said that instead of seeing the current workforce as the sources of the agency's problems, it is necessary to realize that they are the main source of expertise and knowledge about what is going badly and how to fix it. Another vendor said that they try to make their outsourcing contracts pass at least part of the benefit of key incentives on to the workers, while noting that dealing with needed "culture and behavioral change" happened faster and deeper when workers felt they were part of the incoming team rather than the enemy.

Perhaps most telling was former Massachusetts Secretary of Transportation, Fred Salvucci's comment that the standard right-left political arguments for or against contracting totally miss the point. Contrary to most conservative arguments, contracting out simply does not work as a strategy for budget retrenchment without service quality decline. But simply preserving public sector jobs without finding ways to revitalize and expand service is a liberal trap that leaves the agency running an increasingly despised service, undermining the public's faith in government as a whole.

Collaborations

Collaborations describe an even more varied set of usually "one-off," unique contractual or informal arrangements between public agencies and private businesses, foundations, social investors, individual donors, "Friends of..." groups, and other non-profits. When done well, they provide important opportunities for public agencies to expand the range of public value they provide. The non-government partner can provide assets or expertise the public group lacks, can help demonstrate and test new ways of doing things and new things to do, even fill operational or even budgetary gaps.

However, even when the relationship is the result of what is described as a "generous donation" or "gift," they are seldom without cost to the public agency and can easily divert the agency's limited capacity away from its core mission. And even these special arrangements also create endless opportunities for favoritism, mismanagement, and scandal.

Collaborations take many forms. They are each individually negotiated and, at their best, they are win-win propositions. In some situations, a private partner's ability to create ancillary revenue opportunities in a traditionally passive asset (i.e., an offer to set up a café in a park) creates a slew of benefits: new jobs for local people, a service or program that wouldn't otherwise exist, attracting additional people to the area, and perhaps some additional revenue for the public partner, thereby adding to the sustainability of the public resource. Another double win might be giving a school or non-profit a long-term lease and some degree of primary access to a public facility such as a sports field or a theater in exchange for investment in upgrading, maintenance, and operations --while preserving an acceptable level of public use. Often, "Friends" groups are allowed to raise money and oversee some amount of improvements and/or operations/ activity in a public park or other facility – although the Central Park Conservancy inequality problem can easily arise.

Businesses can also play a role. Real estate developers and other businesses are often required to "mitigate" the increased traffic congestion, environmental degradation, or other negative effects of their projects through improvements to a nearby intersection, upgrading of a nearby park or playground, or other compensatory actions. Even when not required to, a business may offer to help pay for, or even build, nearby public improvements or programs that increase the value of their own investments. Business associations or business improvement districts (BIDs) are frequently put in charge of maintaining, programming, and covering the costs of downtown "pocket parks." The owners of the new Encore Casino in Everett, MA are putting many tens of millions of dollars into road improvements, pedestrian bridges, parklands, and other infrastructure – which, however, begs the question of what experience elsewhere has shown to be the negative effects of a gambling venue on vulnerable people and the surrounding areas.

Some offers of help actually do advance the public agency's mission and serve the broadest possible constituency, or free up funds for other needed work without becoming an excuse for future budget cuts. On the other hand, some projects primary benefit a particular (usually well-off) constituency or simply increase the value of the contributor's property or business without providing sufficient value for the general population to justify the public partner's required investment of staff time and other resources. For example, a wealthy donor might offer land adjacent to his estate if the agency creates a land trust – but there is no money to cover the future costs of maintaining the property and no offer to help buy land or help with programming in poor neighborhoods.

A funder's pet project may not fit with the current priority needs and plans of the public agency, or may be focused on a particular subpopulation that is not the agency's constituency of top concern at the current time. It is not always possible for a public agency to change its approved capital budget plans to rebuild one roadway instead of another, or expand sailboat facilities instead of rebuilding children's swings. Even if the arrangement is a mostly "hands-off" relationship supposedly requiring little agency involvement, new programs need supervision and evaluation. The "opportunity cost" to the agency, the diversion of attention from other projects, may be prohibitive.

In addition, on the government side, for collaborations to work the public agency has to have a nontypically efficient decision-making process that is predictable, transparent, flexible, quick, and capable of handling the unpredictable variety of partnership proposals that drop in at unpredictable times in unpredictable numbers. The public agency has to have an internal culture, and the legal authority, that permit its staff to give up some degree of control over its facility operations, programming, and even its long-term investment plans. Agency leaders have to be protected from the legitimate fear that entering into a P3 will open them to attacks for abandoning their agency's responsibilities or for benefiting one constituency over the general public, or that they'll get blamed for the private partner's failures.

Increasing the chances of miscommunication and failure, private partners – especially those bringing money to the table – sometimes assume that their good intentions should overrule public sector rules on permitting and multi-agency approval; that already overburdened staff should drop other responsibilities to analyze and implement their offer. And if things take too long, or don't get resolved in a manner to their liking, the "donors" complain – sometimes publicly, in a tone of entitlement and anger about the incompetence if not stupidity of the public agency's staff.

The New Frontier: Social Investment Entrepreneurs

A lot of creative thought has been put into finding ways that for-profit businesses can promote social good as well as private profit. A huge variety of methods have been developed: fair trade agreements, microfinance, "triple bottom line" B corporations, as well as "philanthrocapitalist" loans, guarantees, investments, and other financial support to social service programs with the return or level of repayment based on the program's ability to use the funds to successfully reduce the societal costs of the issue they are dealing with.

Each of these types of activity have enormous potential and many challenges, from the high interest rates charged by microfinance systems to the narrowness of the measurements used to calculate returns on philanthrocapitalist investments. A few involve public agencies; most are between foundations or individuals and non-profit organizations. But it is a sector worth watching as a new type of Public-Private Partnerships.

Getting To Yes

Advocates have to pay as close attention to the operational details of public-private partnerships as to the broader policy issues. Not all P3s – especially well-constructed collaborations – are bad. Some are huge improvements. But getting to success is difficult.

The ultimate point of any partnership is to create value and the ultimate issue is how to divide that added value (and the risks creating it entails) between the public, the agency, and the private partner. No matter which type of arrangement the public sector uses, these are fundamentally political questions that elected leaders should be required to explain before the public allows them to proceed.

SECTION VI:

MOVING FORWARD

To be hopeful in bad times ... is based on the fact that human history is a history not only of cruelty, but also of compassion, sacrifice, courage, kindness. If we remember those times and places—and there are so many—where people have behaved magnificently, this gives us the energy to act, and at least the possibility of sending this spinning top of a world in a different direction.

HOWARD ZINN

You may never know what results come of your actions; but if you do nothing, there will be no results.

ATTRIBUTED TO MAHATMA GANDHI

15. ADVOCACY AMIDST TURMOIL: Fighting on Two Fronts

15. ADVOCACY AMIDST TURMOIL:
Fighting on Two Fronts

Take a look around you, boy, it's bound to scare you, boy,
But you tell me over and over and over again my friend,
Ah, you don't believe we're on the eve of destruction.

P.F. SLOAN "EVE OF DESTRUCTION" (SUNG BY BARRY
MCGUIRE)

If you close your eyes and open them again, the periodic disintegrations that punctuate our history – all those crumbling ruins – begin to fade, and something else comes into focus: wiliness, stubbornness and, perhaps the strongest and most essential human trait, adaptability.

"HOW DO YOU KNOW WHEN SOCIETY IS ABOUT TO FALL
APART?" BEN ENRENREICH, NYTIMES, 11/4/2020

After 4 years of racist ranting, personal and appointee corruption, and deadly administrative incompetence, over 74 million Americans voted to give Donald Trump four more. Months and years later, a significant percentage of them still believe that Joe Biden's victory was a fraud, that he holds office illegitimately, that victory – and their country -- was stolen from them.

The Republican party is still the home of the roughly one-third of the American population that is driven by some combination of opposition to abortion and immigration, support for gun rights and local negation of federal law, anti-communism, anti-Semitism, Islamophobia, admiration of Trump's unapologetic masculinist bullying, "America First" isolationism, and nationalist white racism. They believe that their right to liberty is God-given; that the only legitimate role of government is to support their use of their property in any way they choose; that taxes are theft; that without guns citizens are defenseless against a government against which armed rebellion is required because it has been taken over by conspiratorial evil forces or turned into a Zionist Occupation Government.

Led by a growing network of right-wing militants, the hard-core

Trumpican base has repeatedly shown their ability and willingness to destroy the career of any Republican who appears insufficiently loyal to the former president. And threatening to vote people out is only the tip of their intimidation. Kim Ward, the Republican majority leader of the Pennsylvania Senate said after the 2020 election: "If I would say to you 'I don't want to do it [support Trump's claims of election fraud]' I'd get my house bombed tonight." (*NYTimes*, 12/920) Keeping it going are continuing inflows of millions of dollars from right-wing businessmen. And Republican gains in 2021 in many down-ballot races gives them the ability to change voting laws in ways that make voting difficult for people of color and to imposing even more flagrant gerrymandering, both of which the right-wing Supreme Court has ruled not subject to federal prevention.

Traditional business conservatives are fighting to regain control of the party they once ran. But it will be difficult. Of the seven GOP Senators who voted for impeachment, most have been repudiated by their state's Republican leadership. Still, it's not clear that business leaders will totally reject their Party. They've already shown that, short of insurrection, they were willing to accept Trump's social policies in exchange for massive tax cuts and deregulation. They may not want Trump, but they have no objection to l reactionary positions. Besides, as Ralph Nader learned, our political system has so deeply baked-in the two-party approach that starting a third is extremely difficult.

A REPUBLICAN FUTURE

Despite their internal conflicts, there are several reasons for Republicans to have long-term confidence. In 2020, despite the Democrats raising more money, the GOP retained federal Senate seats in several states and picked up additional seats in the House of Representatives. Trump's personal style was part of his appeal to the most fanatic of their base; but it turned off others, helping give Biden his margin. However, as shown by the Republicans' continuing nation-wide success in down-ballot races, there was broad support for the party's new mix of core beliefs –

the need in difficult times to first take care of your own, distrust of government, a feeling that national elites don't care about and look down at ordinary people, anxiety about the loss of past status, a demand to deal with insecurity through strength, and the need for public deference to religion.

Further undercutting Democrats' predictions of a demography-driven future majority, Republican candidates attracted a higher-than-ever percentage of African-American, Latinx, and Asian voters in the 2020 election. Despite Trump having spent five years calling immigrants criminal rapists and drug dealers, he won over 30 percent of the vote in all of the heavily Hispanic Texas border counties. And even if non-whites mostly vote Democratic, the overall electorate will remain white-majority for decades to come. Sociologist Richard Alba estimates that in 2060 white voters will still be fifty-five percent of the total. (*The New Yorker*, "The After Party," 11/2/20).

Past experience suggests that, as the opposition party, the GOP is likely to gain congressional seats in the 2022 off-year elections. For mainstream Democrats, now that their orange-haired devil is gone, the enormous anti-Trump outpouring of liberal volunteers and money will probably fade. Grass-roots Republican leaders are embedded in stable, local groups with consistently high election turnouts – churches, private schools, business associations, blue-collar workplaces and local unions – while Liberals' base is among dying mainstream Protestant denominations and ephemeral on-line networks.

Even better, from a Republican perspective, is that the progressive commitment to intersectional rights repeatedly raises culturally divisive issues. As Trump's personal faults fade into the past, Republicans will keep reminding people that until the "Chinese virus" hit, the economy got steadily better during Republican rule, reducing unemployment and raising wages even for those at the bottom.

Contending Trends

All this creates an extremely nourishing sea for armed Alt-right gorillas to swim within. The militant insurrectionists are a loose network of white nationalist militia, Nazi wannabees, KKK and NRA gun clubs, anti-immigrant border vigilantes and INS thugs mixed with right-wing veterans, police groups, and a surprisingly large number of violent conspiracy-believing cultists -- not all of whom are actually mentally ill. Despite their failed coup and the belated FBI attention that has forced them to be more discrete, they are still here and still active.

This is not the first time this country has seen such a development. In the 1840s Know Nothing nativists attacked the arriving Irish, ripping apart the major parties and helping to make room for the new Republican Party. After the Civil War, the Klu Klux Klan burned its way through Reconstruction democracy to bring power back to the Old South's aristocracy, elevating segregationists to power in state and federal governments. In the 1920s, a revived KKK co-existed with militant Catholic anti-Semitism and WASP America-first isolationists; the combination was only able to be pushed to the sidelines by the upsurge of multi-ethnic unions into the New Deal and the coming of war with their fascist friends in Germany and Italy. And now we've again seen that Sinclair Lewis was right: It can happen here. America has a fascist movement.

The Trumpist invasion of Congress was incited by the President, was not stopped by the Capital police, was deliberately allowed to escalate by Trump's Defense Department officials, had the support of a high proportion of elected Republicans at the federal and state levels, and included a great many military veterans with extensive ties to local police. The presence of tens of thousands of Trump supporters gave cover to the core insurrectionists. And there was the apparent magical thinking of so many of those who came to Washington believing in their President's promise to make everything turn out ok. Trump would probably have been happy to accept a successful coup's anointment.

And yet the coup failed. Despite the guns and bombs and hostage-taking equipment they brought, they had to retreat and regroup into the informal networks of armed extremist groups from which they came. Joe Biden and Kamala Harris took office. Not because "the institutions of American democracy saved us." In fact, it was the failures of those systems that allowed Trump and his minions to get as far as they have in multiple areas, from immigration to voter suppression, from environmental/climate devastation to public health disasters, and so much more.

One reason the coup failed was the lack of military support, partly due to the top brass' fury at Trump's incompetent bungling, repeated insults, and obvious instability. The business world's concerns about Trump's increasing irrationality in the face of an exploding pandemic, and their fear of national upheaval should the election results be ignored, also played a role. In addition, the uniquely fragmented, decentralized, and uncoordinated structure of American government into thousands of separately elected branches and chambers and states and cities kept the plotters from a coordinated national push. It also allowed some state and local officials to resist Trump's demands in the name of personal integrity and respect for past practices.

But underlying it all was the massive mobilization of anti-Trump forces -- particularly including southern African-American women whose outpouring provided the margin of victory in swing states -- whose forceful presence set the deeper context for the refusal of just enough public officials to surrender to the Trumpite's efforts to overthrow the vote. The nation-wide outburst of celebration by Biden supporters after the election made it clear that they weren't going away. It was the visible base of support for democracy that was the foundation for the insurrection's inability to get past the first stage.

Pushing Democracy

Now the strategic progressive imperative is to use the crises to expand and strengthen democracy – protecting voting rights, expanding access to the polls, reducing the influence of big money, and eliminating gerrymandering. One part of that effort is exposing the presence and power of the far right, and demanding their removal – while avoiding our own political marginalization by publicly and repeatedly re-affirming a strategic commitment to democracy and non-violence. Seeking out and physically attacking militia groups is a prescription for political suicide. We should leave confront-and-arrest tasks to the FBI and police. (On the other hand, it is not a contradiction to say that we should learn from the Civil Rights movement that its sometimes helpful for vigilantes to know that we are able to protect ourselves from violent attacks if necessary.)

Another component of bettering democracy is building broad coalitions to demand we live up to the best of our national ideals. This means working with people and groups that we may differ with or even strongly oppose on other issues. Progressives have to recognize the difference between coalitions composed of people and groups who only agree on a specific and limited set of demands and actions, and partnerships which require a deeper and broader compatibility around perspective and goals.

At a minimum, winning democratic reform requires a working relationship with what remains of liberalism in state and national governments. As Bernie Sanders, Alexandria Ocasio-Cortez, Ayanna Pressley, and the rest of the "Squad" have shown, progressives can operate within the Democratic party by treating liberals as allies with whom they argue rather than as enemies with whom they are at war. It may even be possible, for certain issues, to shape demands in ways that conservatives can also support – the way some aspects of prison reform became bipartisan after right-wingers began going to jail.

All this requires a certain real-world pragmatism. In *The New Climate War*, Michael Mann says we must avoid the "friendly fire" of political "purists" who posit everything in all-or-nothing terms that leave us with little but doom, and to never fall into the trap of believing it's too late to make things better.

In addition, just as Trump's allies have shown themselves willing to use every trick they can, progressives need to accept that the path to victory requires using every type of influence -- arm twisting and deal-making as much as moral suasion. At the height of the Civil War, the nation adopted the first constitutional guarantee of citizenship at both the federal and state levels for all people "born or naturalized in the United States." Sherman was burning through Georgia and Grant was destroying Petersburg. Union military victory was in sight. The Confederacy was falling. And yet, even at this moment of maximum power, the 13th Amendment ending slavery was only passed by Congress because of bribes, job offers, and other back-room deals. And the required approval by three-quarters of the states was only achieved by the legal maneuver of excluding Southern states from the total needed despite the Civil War's legal justification that succession was not allowed. (This is the basis for the contemporary claim by some right-wing jurists that the 13th Amendment is not a "primary" part of the Constitution!)

More recently, we know that even in the midst of the Civil Rights Movement and despite the motivating shock of John Kennedy's assassination, Lyndon Johnson needed brutal levels of arm-twisting threats, secret trades, and payoffs to pass the 1964 Civil Rights bill. Progress requires the coming together of many forces pushing from both the bottom and the top and does not get built with clean hands.

Falling In A Hole

The Biden victory has brought back into office many veterans of the same Clinton-Obama neo-liberal subservience to high finance that laid the groundwork for Trump's initial rust-belt based victory. Centrist "New Economy" Democrats, no less than their "New World Order" Republican counterparts, have shaped American and international markets to weaken workers' bargaining power, facilitate outsourcing both domestically and internationally, promote price-based free trade exchanges, reduce anti-trust and business regulation, and facilitate the dominance of financial capitalism.

All this leaves individuals, and regions, increasingly vulnerable to more powerful players; leading -- as an inherent dynamic in all unequal market relationships – to the transfer of wealth and power to the already dominant. There is a geographic component, that partly explains Trump's appeal in various regions.

Once, wealth and prosperity were spread out across the country. In the 1960s, the 25 cities with the highest median incomes included Cleveland, Des Moines, Milwaukee and Rockford, Ill. By the middle of the last decade, virtually all of the top 25 were on the coasts. Meanwhile, the gap between wealthy and poorer regions has grown much wider. In 1980, only a few sections of the country had median incomes that were more than 20 percent above or below the national average. Today, big chunks of the country fall into those extremes. The imbalance is unhealthy at both ends of the spectrum. In one set of places, it produces congestion and unaffordability; on the other, blight and stagnation. "Amazon and the Breaking of Baltimore," by Alec MacGillis, NYTimes, 3/9/21)

The domestic effects were one manifestation of a global system. *Since the late 20th century, capitalist globalization has increasingly adopted the form of interlinked commodity chains controlled by multinational corporations, connecting various production zones, primarily in the Global South, with the center of world consumption, finance, and accumulation, primarily in the Global North. In this system, exorbitant profits are made not only from global labor arbitrage, through which multinational corporations overexploit industrial labor, but also increasingly through global land arbitrage, in which agri-business multinationals expropriate cheap land in the Global South so as to produce export crops mainly for sale in the Glo-bal North.* ("Covid 19 and Catastrophe Capitalism," John Bellamy Foster and Intan Suwandi, Dollars & Sense, Jan/ Feb 2021)

For the past forty years income and wealth have moved up-wards, the percentage of temporary and part-time jobs without benefits has increased, and the number of families in poverty or homeless has grown. The neo-liberal undermining of working-class America's living standards, combined with the repeated push-back by non-white developing nations and movements against American power, has created enormous insecurity among a white working class that had previously experienced two generations of prosperity. Rather than abandon the en-tire American myth that hard work leads to success, men and women in both declining rural and abandoned industrial areas have focused their resentment – and growing anger -- on the cultural changes and populations identified with those changes that seem to question their traditional perception of self-worth

In particular, they've developed an envious yet infuriated feel-ing about the mainstream mass media whose programs and advertisements present prosperous, non-religious, college-edu-cated, young professionals living in cool, upscale coastal cities and an increasingly visible number of formerly invisible types of people as the high-status version of the new reality. The na-tional Democratic Party's courting of those same groups at the expense of its former centering of mainstream ethnic families becomes another source of hurt. Of course, the desire to keep America as it was feeds into every traditional prejudice against "outsiders" and "others" as well as the conservative/libertarian push to weaken governmental intervention in both social rela-tionships and markets.

Reviewing *The Tyranny of Merit*, by Michael Sandel, Elizabeth

Anderson writes in *The Nation* (3, 8-15, 2021):

> *The top tier of workers -- highly educated, cosmopolitan class of professional, knowledge, and culture workers -- has turned itself into a self-reproducing elite.... while the losers feel humiliated, continually told they deserve the fate to which elites consign them. However socially necessary their jobs may be, their contributions to the common good are disparaged by elites as uncredentialed and 'low skill.' This adds insult to the injury of stagnant wages and precarity that many working-class Americans face... In stressing education as the primary means to get ahead in society, the [Democratic] party's educated elites have come to offer an increasingly narrow pathway to a decent life... [which] leads to a politics of resentment.*

But the Republican Party has much broader support than among blue-collar and rural families. Small business owners, suburban housewives, and devout Christains also find the GOP message relevant to their discomforts. Republican pollster Kristen Soltis Anderson notes that Donald Trump expressed and legitimized the escalation of their fury at elites and their desire for ways to explosively fight back.

> *One of the most unifying beliefs of the Trump coalition was the idea that there is religious persecution of Christians in the U.S. these days... [He was] going to defend their right to practice their religion as they saw fit and not be told —not just by government, but by other institutions — by schools that their children go to, or by the media, by their employers that they're not allowed to hold certain beliefs.... that is increasingly why you see so many on the right talking about things like cancel culture.*

Finding An Opportunity

It's important to remember that a majority of those with incomes below $100,000 favored Biden, while those with incomes over $100,000 favored Trump. This opens a huge strategic opportunity for progressives, who need to counter-balance their center-leaning alliances with a dramatic strengthening of their own base. Hopefully, there is a component of the original Trump electoral majority that is not stuck in racist anger or other non-negotiable hatreds, and that can even be won to progressive positions around enough issues to consider switching parties again. Some percentage of Republican votes came from people who are not self-consciously racist, do not condone vigilante violence, the complete privatization of all public programs, or the total deregulation of the economy, much less fascism. They agree with many specific Democratic proposals for improved health care, minimum wage increases, environmental protection, and more. They are furious at the corporate billionaires who get rich at everyone else's expense. Many even agree that African-Americans have suffered discrimination in the past and aren't doing so well today.

These are the people who voted for Bernie Sanders in 2016, before they got swept up in Trump's anger and then enmeshed in the full-spectrum of right-wing politics on Fox News and conspiracy-spouting websites. Although harder now than in 2016, it is still possible to wean them away from the GOP.

CLASS CONSCIOUSNESS
Reconnecting with those parts of middle America still open to discussion will require addressing their needs and speaking to their feelings. These are the people whose life experience is of personal and family struggles with economic insecurity, feelings of cultural disrespect, and deep understanding that personal effort is a key factor in life experience. Their thoughts are full of their kids and families, their jobs and communities, their friends and their health.

Biden's famous empathy is a good beginning, but it's not enough. It's true that the size of the grassroots mobilization that swept the new Administration to victory and the depth of the crises that Trump has exacerbated, has pushed Biden into more aggressive and progressive positions than his history would have predicted. But the limits of his vision are tight, and will increasingly become clear. Progressives need to push beyond those limits to advocate and organize for more. This requires expanding the electorate by fighting for increased electoral access and supporting the self-mobilization of African-Americans and other previously marginalized groups. But that will not be enough for solid majorities. It will also require gaining support from white working-class families and non-urban communities.

While liberals talk about rebuilding the social safety net, progressives have to push for "pre-distributive" policies that shape the economy to produce a more equal distribution of resources even before taxes or public programs kick in. Policies that strengthen and expand union organizing, raise the minimum wage, improve workplace and consumer safety standards, reduce barriers to business and professional entry, increase anti-trust enforcement, and more. This doesn't eliminate the need for a safety net, but does make people less likely to need it.

To be heard, progressive advocacy organizing will also have to reshape its own language and demands. There must be a more explicit emphasis on rebuilding the manufacturing industry and other "good" jobs as well as unions, on revitalizing rural areas as well as cities, on supporting families as well as individuals. In addition, as Elizabeth Warren made clear, American populism has historically included support for small businesses. In the US context, small business – like property ownership -- is an aspirational route to upward mobility and family stability for working families, particularly immigrants. Progressives need to champion a thriving small business economy as a potential counter to the increased concentration in most industries.

RACIAL PERSPECTIVES
Most controversially, without reducing pressure for ending institutional racism and sexism along with continued support for a total re-vamping of how social peace and policing are

done, progressives have to stop calling the majority of white people racist. Of course, it's true that most of Western prosperity, and therefore its cultural consciousness, was built on the exploitation of violently oppressed people at the bottom of various hierarchies: displaced peasants, immigrants, women and children, and most drastically non-Europeans, particularly Africans. It's true that slavery and racism are intimately intertwined with the entire history of this country and a major source of its current wealth. It's true that most white people are spared the police treatment, daily insults, and economic marginality of most African-Americans.

However, very few white people consciously see their daily lives as racially defined, and don't see their political choices as having much to do with racial issues. They know that their own grandparents were persecuted in the "old country," and were brutally treated when they arrived here. But neither their immigrant forbearers nor they themselves have any consciousness or experience of being generationally privileged – including racial privilege. Yes: in fact, structurally there are many ways in which they are. But it will be impossible to get them to adopt this perspective if the first statement they hear is that they are racist – in our society, that term is not a "neutral" or "objective" structural descriptor of "impersonal" institutional processes; it is a personal insult.

Shifting people's understanding of their position in American society starts by acknowledging the legitimacy of their current perspective, by taking their issues and angst seriously, and by helping them adopt strategies that address their own needs in the context of working with a broad range of others – including those worse off and marginalized. It is on the basis of shared struggles and unifying victories that people are able – and willing – to change their deeper frames of reference. And the willingness to enter a common struggle does not come from guilt, but from the desire for and belief in the possibility of a better future.

None of this diminishes the reality of racism. Heather McGhee, in her new book, The Sum of Us: What Racism Costs Everyone and How We Can Prosper Together, points out that most white people will express support for "big public solutions" until the opposition starts framing it as a program that will benefit racial minorities, at which point their support for public goods collapses. Changing these people's perspective by saying they should reject their white privileges is useless: "You have to have an oddly high opinion of white people to assume that most will react to learning about the advantages of whiteness by wanting to give it up." Instead, Ms. McGhee says we need to focus on how racism also hurts white people. Her foundational story is how towns...

> closed their public pools rather than share them with Black people, [protecting the racial hierarchy but] leaving everyone who couldn't afford a private pool materially worse off...Why is student debt so crushing in a country that once had excellent universities that were cheap or even free? Why is American health care such a disaster? Why is our democracy being strangled by minority rule? ... Racism is a huge part of the answer... McGhee describes a "solidarity dividend" gained when people are able to transcend racism... [Raphael Warnock won just enough white voters in Georgia] by appealing to idealism, but also to self-interest. ("The Book That Should Change How Progressives Talk About Race" by Michelle Goldberg, NYTimes 2/19/2021)

The way to begin doing this is balancing the current Trump-stimulated obsession on national politics with a stronger focus on local issues. An effective step in this direction is the adoption of "deep canvassing" – a process of non-judgmental, respectful, and unhurried listening to people of differing perspectives as they talk about emotionally significant experiences relating to public issues, leading to better mutual understanding of (often similar) core values and identification of areas of agreement. If coupled with a commitment to make local issues an advocacy priority in ways that incorporate an awareness of disparate experiences within local populations – it might be possible to build a strong, stable, progressive base capable of tipping the Democratic Party's internal balance of power to the left.

And The Opportunity

People, even entire populations, stuck in unpleasant or even brutal conditions will gripe and quietly resist, but don't usually openly rebel against effectively dominant rulers -- until a viable opportunity for change seems to present itself: the forces of change seem strong, the rulers seem unusually weak. Populist movements, from the right or the left, are a signal that the ruling elites have lost the acquiescence of their subordinate populations, that the dominant world view promulgated by their governors is no longer hegemonic.

In this context, the rise of right-wing populism is an opening for progressive advocates as well. The influx of new activists from a variety of demographic sectors has broadened the type and reach of potential alliances. Right-wing attacks on voting and constitutional rights and democratic processes, particularly their increasing militance about refusing to give up power even after election losses, allows progressives to act as upholders of traditional values and practices. It provides a legitimizing framework for demands for improved vote-counting security, re-imposed oversight of state voter registration rules, and other civil rights measures.

Republican-imposed cuts to our already inadequate social safety net is hurting larger swaths of working families – among whom are an increasing number of the formerly better-employed who previously found no way to express their anger except through Trump, but might be open to a re-orientation if it was attentive to their needs and seemed potentially successful. Across the US, workers and unions have increased their militancy. Stagnating wages and worsening working conditions sent more people out on strike in 2019 than in any of the previous 23 years.

The idea of a Green New Deal has unified much of the environmental and climate movements around a broadened "Thrive agenda." Ironically, Trump's undermining of the US's world position while increasing the military budget and setting the stage for space wars, opens the door for discussion of how to create an ally-friendly collaborative foreign policy backed up by non-imperialist, humanitarian interventions -- a precondition for the drastic reductions of military spending needed to fund progressive reforms.

A progressive resurgence requires going deeper than pocketbook issues. As these notes have emphasized, the vision of an inclusive, democratic, prosperous, safe, and peaceful United States must be based on a strong set of values – dignity for all, respect for every group's history and struggles and successes, a balancing of personal responsibility with social support informed by previous injustices, honest admission of past mistakes and current facts. Progressives need to find ways to acknowledge that the gut-level starting point of most people – to prioritize the well-being of their own family, town, country – is not inherently unethical or an expression of hatred. What turns that legitimate expression of belonging into racism or xenophobia is the historical and political context in which it gets played out – and it is the job of progressives to create movements that provide a healthier context than the Trumpian GOP. Just as important: to be successful, neither close-to-home advocacy or national movements can be expressed as anti-Americanism – we need to find and enunciate appreciation for those parts of our nation's history, values, social and political practices which form the foundation for our current efforts.

We are unlikely to win everything we and the nation needs. No matter who controls the White House and Congress, we are living in a new era in which climate change and recurring pandemics are reshaping our options. But there is a good chance that, along with extremely hard fights, we will create a better world. No matter what, if we each rise to the maximum level of engagement and leadership we can provide, we'll have no regrets -- and, hopefully, a place our children and grandchildren can live in.

ABOUT THE AUTHOR

Steven E. Miller

Steven Miller is a life-long progressive organizer. Starting in high school then continuing through college, he was active in
Civil Rights and anti-war efforts. He gradu-
ated into community organizing -- ten-
ants, welfare, low-income food coops, and regional anti-highway campaigns as well as anti-racism coalitions during Boston's
busing violence.

He helped create the state-wide, union-affiliated Mass Coalition
for Occupational Safety and Health (MassCOSH), hosted a labor-
sponsored radio interview show, and led a seminar on Labor
History. Teaching led to curriculum development at Education Development Center writing about affirmative action, Native American treaty rights, and immigration. He also served as
Board Chair for GrassRoots International, providing support for
Third World movements.

Seeking to democratize access to computing power, Miller was
hired by a high-tech start-up (Lotus Development Corporation),
working on the prize-winning User Manuals, then serving as
Editor-in-Chief of the user-group magazine, as well as helping
found the corporate philanthropy program. He was recruited to
the national board of Computer Professionals for Social Responsibility (CPSR) and wrote his first book – "Civilizing Cyberspace:
Policy, Power, and the Information Superhighway" (Addison-
Wesley). He also served as the on-air Science and Technology

commentator for a national cable channel's premier news show.

After a stint in a state IT agency, Miller organized Massachusetts' NetDay – a campaign to use technology as a tool for project-based, student-centered education. Over 20,000 people across Massachusetts in nearly 3/4s of the state's school districts joined the effort. In Boston, Miller was the founding Board Chair of Tech Boston Academy pilot school, recognized in a site visit by President Obama as a national model.

Shifting to public health and active transportation, he co-founded Boston's Hub On Wheels bicycle festival and was a founding Board member of LivableStreets Alliance, advocating for healthier transportation. During his 15 years at LSA, Miller published a monthly blog: "The Public Way: Transportation, Health, and Livable Communities".

Miller now focuses on supporting his three grandchildren, organizes around climate issues with 350 Mass and other groups, and volunteers with Movement Voter Project (MVP) to raise funds for grass-roots community organizations in strategic local and state elections.